⊲ T5-CCK-344

When
Messiah
Comes

When Messiah Comes

PAUL F. HEGELE

SERMONS FOR
LENT AND EASTER

C.S.S. Publishing Co., Inc.
Lima, Ohio

WHEN MESSIAH COMES

"When Messiah Comes": Music by Jerry Bock, lyrics by Sheldon Harnick.

Copyright © 1986 by
The C.S.S. Publishing Company, Inc.
Lima, Ohio

All rights reserved. No part of this publication may be reproduced, stored in a retrieval system, or transmitted in any form or by any means, electronic, mechanical, photocopying, recording, or otherwise, without the prior permission of the publisher. Inquiries should be addressed to: The C.S.S. Publishing Company, Inc., 628 South Main Street, Lima, Ohio 45804.

6832 / ISBN 0-89536-823-4

PRINTED IN U.S.A.

Table of Contents

*Dedicated to Arlene Smith,
the teacher who taught me
intolerance —
of shoddy reasoning,
dull language
and wasted words.*

Author's Preface

"When Messiah comes . . ." says Tevye, wistfully, in a song written for the Broadway musical *Fiddler On The Roof.* "When Messiah comes and his reign begins truth and justice then shall appear on earth . . . and everything will be all right."

But what about the long days before Messiah comes? How do we cope? In what do we hope?

These sermons are about people waiting and looking for a God they cannot see: Abraham, setting out for a Promised Land; Ezekiel, dreaming God can rebuild his chosen people from a valley of dry bones; Peter, on Pentecost, remembering Christ and promising his return.

These sermons are about people finding strength and making sense out of life in the in-between time before Messiah comes. These sermons are about us.

Joel 2:1-2, 12-17a   *Ash Wednesday*

A New Plan for Lent

The year — 1979. The place — New Orleans.

There's no joy in this town today. Mighty Mardi Gras has struck out. The police are on strike! Parades are canceled. Visitors are not visiting, citizens not celebrating.

No one laughs, no one revels, no one is even tipsy, let alone drunk. Is this any way to begin Lent — somber and sober? Businessmen are giving up their profits for Lent because of lack of customers. Families are tightening their belts, picking at meager meals, afraid, without police, to venture to the supermarket, let alone risk a restaurant. Is this any way to begin Lent — hapless and hungry?

Of course it is. It's precisely the quiet, reflective way Lent should be observed. But before we chuckle at the irony, perhaps we should ask — on whom is the joke? Is it on the people who love the reveling of Mardi Gras? Or, is it on the faithful of the church, you and me, who let Mardi Gras grow to its present proportions, detached from Lent, overshadowing Lent? We have watched this become a misguided, cockeyed season. The fabric of these weeks before Easter, a fabric carefully woven by the early church, has become threadbare and ripped over the years: our efforts to mend it, with little rituals of pancake dinners on this day, and forsaking sweets in Lent, and psyching ourselves up for sunrise on Easter, are little more than a patch job. What's needed is a determination to reweave our season of Lent with the knowledge of how it originally looked.

In the early life of the church, of course, Easter was the Alpha and the Omega of the church year, the season when a Christian's faith and spirit were reborn. The season of Lent existed solely in the shadow of the cross and the empty grave. Lent had two purposes — to prepare Christians for the Easter celebration and to test Christians to learn if they sufficiently appreciated the gift of Easter. Catechumens took their final exam before being baptized on Easter night; the most publicly sinful people made their confessions in front of other Christians; in worship, the Gospel readings dwelt on all the demonic challenges to Christ — Satan in the desert, for instance, and the healing of the possessed — to demonstrate what evil Christ was overcoming on Easter. It was a harsh season, not because of artificial restrictions, but because it was a harsh life of persecutions and living in a decaying society. Yet it was also an eager season because of the Easter joy Christians anticipated: they knew it could rise above the harshness.

The first changes in this simple, strong fabric of Easter and Lent came in the fourth century. Christianity suffered a blow from which it never recovered — it became legitimate in the eyes of the state. The harshness of persecution gave way to respectability. Life for Christians became comfortable. "A new preparation for Easter was needed" the bishops said, "A new testing of faith." Enter — fasting, the means of fortifying the spiritual by depriving the physical. Enter — Lenten offerings, through which Christians, new and old, proved their devotion by sacrificing some of the necessities of life. Enter also the forty-day observance of Lent, up gradually from an original period of two days, on the theory that if the *depth* of a Christian's anguish was no longer great, the *length* of it could still be.

Within a few hundred years, the fabric of the Christian calendar's spring season was changed. The natural flow from Lenten intensity to Easter joy became marked with artificial seams, human requirements of preparations for joy and demonstrations of faith.

The Mardi Gras, at which we scoffed earlier, came from this time. It was a patch sewn on for decoration. The feast of Mardi Gras is a preparation for Lent as surely as Lent is a preparation for Easter. It's a happy day, meant to brace us for harsh days. And it literally was a feast. Mardi Gras is French for "Fat Tuesday." In Italian, the word is "Carnival," meaning, "farewell to meats." Others call it Pancake Tuesday, which is the English, meaning, "Let's use up all the eggs and milk, for tomorrow they'll be pitched."

From Easter morning to Lent to Mardi Gras, the fabric of this season is unrolled, to be trampled and bunched and torn.

Don't we need the same deepening of devotion the early Christians sought? You and I need the same emphasis on the spiritual, the same preparation for Easter. But I fear, in Lent, as we know it, this discipline is twisted beyond recognition. When many bemoaned the loss of one Mardi Gras, while few remember what it meant in the first place, something's wrong. When many talk about repenting sins, while few do it, apart from stale confessions or whipping themselves into a psychological frenzy, something's wrong.

Why don't we do away with some of the old trappings of Lent? Our ancestors did away with flagellations — self-whippings — 600 years ago. People no longer have themselves nailed to a cross in memory of Christ. Why don't we do away with the practices which are outdated for our time.

Do away with practices such as special offerings as a Lenten sacrifice. Few people today discipline the body by giving a few extra coins to the church. The day when an extra offering is a real sacrifice, *good for the soul,* is long past. We are too wealthy to deprive ourselves so easily. All the little offering does is make a person think they have bought God's favor, plus nourishing our love for wealthy churches.

Let's, also, forget this emphasis on fasting. In this age, when doctors estimate the average American is fourteen pounds overweight, going without food doesn't indicate devotion to God, but devotion to a sexy figure. Going without food is not cause for remorsing, but cause for rejoicing because it means the approach of slimness, attractiveness. We call it dieting, which comes from the Greek word for *promoting health.*

We need some other penance, something else to feed our souls while it disciplines our bodies; something else which will prepare us for Easter.

If we're serious about growing spiritually during Lent, why don't we observe it by living among the poor for awhile. Perhaps you've heard of the college president in Tennessee who spends his summers working with the poor, clandestinely. He sweeps streets and washes dishes. He says he wants to better understand how the other half lives. It costs him — pride, clean hands, and good clothes. But he's paid back in wisdom and humility. Couldn't we find the same reward by volunteering at a soup kitchen for the poor or at the county welfare agency?

If you want to grow spiritually, why don't you do volunteer work at a local hospital or at CONTACT, the crisis phone service; volunteers are always eagerly sought. Placed as a volunteer among the anguished and the dying, our concerns about boredom on the job and the lack of direction in life seem petty. All that counts, in such work, is how well you can love and serve another. It's a great chance to learn about people, including yourself.

If these sound too demanding, why not observe Lent simply by practicing to speak of your faith, to speak of it honestly, lovingly, sensitively. It's so easy for us to view witnessing to our faith as merely handing out brochures and living an upright life, without ever explaining to our neighbors what makes us upright. Why not take the risk of encouraging another to speak of his pursuit of God, and then humbly speaking of our own. Certainly, witnessing to one's struggle in faith can be as humbling and chastising as any fast. And it's far better preparation for Easter. After all, what is the Easter Gospel but a series of stories about witnessing: Jesus telling Mary he really is alive, the disciples discussing whether reports are true, doubting Thomas and the men going to Emmaus, talking about fear and faith. What better use of Lent then preparing to emulate the Easter characters by daring to talk about personal faith?

The old ways of observing Lent are as torn from the fabric of this season as is Mardi Gras. We need new challenges to deepen our faith, new insights to prepare us for Easter. Finding them can be our task. And if, in this pursuit, we struggle humbled, bewildered, beset, so much the better. After all, that's what Lent is about.

The Ladder of Success

The window into my childhood sometimes opens for me. I can catch glimpses of scenes from the past. The image most vivid is of two small boys — my best friend and me — sitting on the steps of my back porch. Our conversation is always the same. It begins when one asks the other: "What are you going to be when you grow up?"

The answers then are much like the answers children give today. "What do you want to be when you grow up?" A cowboy, a teacher, a football player, a doctor.

Being Superman was my personal ambition, at least until that black day of maturity, when he went the way of Santa Claus and the tooth fairy.

Astronauts had not yet been invented. Even our parents didn't know what a paramedic was.

The answers we gave changed as we grew older, but the question never left. I think it's still true today. Of course, a mother has to drop the words, "when you grow up," on the day a daughter announces she has a *steady boy* or on the day the basketball team measures her son at six feet. And, of course, when we become adults, the question, "What are you going to be?" comes disguised in different words. But it's still there.

What is your major?

Which job offer will you take?

Are you hoping for a transfer?

Are you going to run for the school board . . . PTA . . . church council . . . board of directors?

We measure our lives by the answers we give to those questions.

The trouble is, there's no end to asking the question. "What are you going to be?" One day the child will answer "cowboy," the next day, "fireman." Eventually, he/she becomes a doctor. But the question keeps chasing them. "What are you going to be?" Not just a doctor, but a surgeon; not just a surgeon, but a skilled and famous surgeon; not just a successful surgeon, but one who sits on the board of directors of the hospital, who writes books, who leads this profession. As long as there's breath in our bodies, the thought, "What more can I be?" taunts us. The name of the game is success. We either *climb* the ladder or we *get off*.

Up or off. That's not much of a choice. What happens to the people who do *get off*, who decide climbing the ladder is too hard or is no longer possible?

The playwright, Arthur Miller, paints a stark picture of such a person. The play is "Death of a Salesman." It's a play about Willie Loman's self-image. At the play's beginning, Willie Loman sees himself as a friendly, popular salesman, with as many good stories to his credit as big sales. At the play's mid-point, though, he knows that he is merely a salesman — his friends don't need him, his company can't promote him. By the play's end, he's killed himself.

To "get out of the race" is to try to avoid the tempest by crawling down onto the ledge of a crevice; we hope we don't fall all the way. The feeling becomes more frequent the older we get, the shorter our future becomes. How many of you middle-aged men want an early retirement?

To want to get off the ladder of success is to bow to the fact that, as the world counts achievement, most of us will not be greatly successful. We live in homes, not mansions, and we control businesses, not corporations. So we seek contentment in the limited success we do find in life.

But let's be honest with ourselves. Such contentment is little more than a consolation prize. If it were simply up to our wishes — our hopes — whether we go far up the ladder of success or get off, then we had better be prepared for a fast, steep climb. How many of you would not like to change places with your boss, or with your boss's boss?

The more we look at that ladder, the more we realize ambition is at the base of human motives.

That's not a new fact. The power of ambition was known to our ancestors in faith 5000 years ago. They spoke of it when they composed the Old Testament lesson for today — the fall in Eden. Let us remind ourselves again that the first part of the Bible was written not to record primitive history; stories early in the Bible were created by the Hebrews to help explain the world as they saw it, a world racked by evil but in the hands of a just God. So it is with the story of the Fall.

The world of early Genesis included Adam, Eve, a lot of animals, and paradise. It doesn't include sin or suffering. The only rule of life is that the tree in the center of the garden of Eden, the tree of the knowledge of good and evil, is not to be touched. And what happens? You know it. The snake whispers to Eve, "If you eat of that tree, you will be as gods." Then ambition takes over. Living in Eden wasn't enough; Adam saw some room on the top rung of the success ladder and he jumped at it. The result? God gave our couple an eviction notice. Ambition, driven by greed, leads to disaster.

And yet we need to be careful here. Because nowhere in our faith is there the concept all ambition is bad. Some ambition, in fact, is very good.

It's an irony of the Bible that the people who composed the story of the Fall were themselves very ambitious. Their ambition was to gain a type of mastery of the world by explaining all they saw in the world. Therefore:

> A loving God makes men work for a living because Adam was
> kicked out of this paradise;
> Women have pain in childbirth as punishment for Eve
> tempting Adam;
> Snakes have to crawl instead of walk because one of them
> prompted Eve to disobey God.

By explaining the world, by putting things of nature in their place, ancient man destroyed the fear born of ignorance. He stepped forth confidently as master of a world no longer strange to him.

And God said such ambition was good. "Fill the earth and subdue it" is his command; "rule over . . . every living thing that moves upon the earth. Give every living creature a name that you choose."

Ambition can be good. Imagine a world where no one was ambitious, where no one thought of accomplishments and improvements. Cartoonist Charles Schultz allows us to glimpse such a world in the words of Lucy, one of his characters in Peanuts. Lucy tells Charlie Brown she doesn't yet know what to do with herself during summer vacation. Charlie Brown's advice? "Start a new hobby. The people who get the most out of life are those who really try to accomplish something." "Accomplish something," says Lucy, "I thought we were just supposed to keep busy."

The desire to be successful can be good. The trouble starts, though, when we want too much success. The trouble starts because, no matter how far up the ladder of success we climb, we want to go higher. Given a Garden of Eden, we still want to be "as Gods." Janitors want to be foremen, foremen want to be managers, managers want to be chairmen of the board. Think of the Sunday afternoon artist who secretly hopes to become a professional painter. But the professional painter dreams of having her painting in museums. And the artist whose works are in a museum longs to be called a new Picasso. I don't even dare mention the ambition of a buck private in the army. He would need eighteen promotions in rank before he could become the top general.

All of us share some of this sin of Adam, this self-centeredness which can make us a slave to our ambitions. The more enslaved to that ambition we become, the keener the pain when we fail to reach the top.

Imagine, for a moment, what it would be like if we did make it to the top; if, instead of getting off the ladder of success exhausted, we actually climbed to the highest rung.

The ancients thought of that, too. One place it is spoken of is in an old Japanese children's story, the parable of Tapu. Let's share this familiar story again.

Tapu was a very average farmer. Each day he would walk past his wife and children, past his animals and barn, and into the fields where he planted his crop. Sometimes Tapu became very tired of this common life. He would wonder, "Why must I go on planting and reaping, planting and reaping? Why can't I become someone else, someone greater?"

One day, while he was working away in the field, Tapu heard footsteps. He looked out to the road and saw the king riding past in his carriage and surrounded by his servants.

Tapu thought: "How fine to be a king! If only I could be a king in a carriage with my servants behind me." Then he began to chant:

"The king, the king,
the king I would be."

A voice said "Tapu, be the king!"

Tapu became a king and sat on a great horse with servants following behind him. And Tapu said, "I am the king and no one in the world is greater than I." But soon a messenger came to Tapu and told him an enemy was invading the country and his kingdom was about to fall. Then Tapu became angry and said, "Is there someone greater than a king?" And he began to chant:

> "The soldier, the soldier,
> the soldier I would be."

The voice said: "Tapu, be the soldier!"

Then Tapu became a soldier — a general — with his troops all around him. He gave many orders every day. But a scholar — a philosopher — appeared in the land. He made speeches to the people and told them they could be something more in life than slaves to the soldiers. And the people rebelled. Then Tapu became angry and said, "Is there someone greater than a general?" And he began to chant:

> "The scholar, the scholar,
> the scholar I would be."

The voice said: "Tapu, be the scholar!"

Then Tapu became a scholar — a philosopher — and he sat on a rock and thought great thoughts. He thought about why the world was as it is and why people do the things they do. But soon, the thoughts stopped coming to him. He no longer saw much of the world or the people in it. He no longer saw the basics of life as simple men can. Then Tapu became angry and said "Is there someone greater than a scholar?" And he began to chant:

> "The man, the man,
> the simple man I would be."

And the voice said: "Tapu, be yourself!"

Be yourself. Such simple advice. Beware of being a slave to ambition. Climb the ladder of success if you want, but don't try to make a mad scramble of it. Why? Because the ladder leads nowhere. It has no top. Simple man to king to general to scholar to simple man. A chairman of the board has as many bosses as there are stockholders in his company. The child who dreams of being a cowboy knows someday even this dream cowboy will meet a gunfighter faster than himself.

No matter how high we go on the ladder, we don't think it's high enough. No matter how much worth we feel our position in life gives us, there's the nagging doubt, "Am I worthy enough?"

Self-acceptance is hard. That's the lesson Adam learned. God said to Adam: "Now, look, remember who you are. You have importance, you have worth, because I made you and I love you. Don't try to be someone other than my child." And Adam promptly decided to be the god of his own life. Having the worth of being a child whom God loves wasn't enough; Adam wanted the greatness of standing on the top rung of the ladder. Looking at the tree in the center of the garden, Adam knew he had a choice. He made the wrong choice and he discovered sin, suffering, and shame.

The choice didn't stop with Adam. It keeps popping up in history, in every generation and in every life. The choice confronted Christ. "Renounce your sonship to God and worship me" said the devil, "and I will give you the world."

The difference between what Christ chose and what Adam chose is explained by St. Paul in today's Epistle. Because of Adam "death reigned through that one man." But those who choose "the abundance of grace and the free gift of righteousness offered by God will reign in life."

Look for your worth by scrambling up the ladder of success. Or recognize the worth — the "reign in life" — which we have as children of God.

That's the choice which faced Adam.

That's the choice which faced Christ.

That's the choice facing us.

Two boys sat on the steps of the back porch. One asked the other: "What do you want to be when you grow up?"

A Wandering Aramean

Ten years ago history was made in the broadcast of a television show. The show was *Roots*. As you may remember, *Roots* was a documentary of one man's search for his ancestry. Black author, Alex Haley's hunger to know his identity led him to record his own roots, his own heritage, first on paper, then on the screen. And the significance of this T.V. show? This mini-series attracted more viewers than any other television program in history. With eighty-five million viewers, this story of the black man's struggle in the Old South easily surpassed the former record-holder for an audience, a show which, ironically enough, portrayed the *white man's supremacy* in the Old South — the famous movie *Gone With The Wind*.

Of course, the audience record set by Alex Haley's story is not the greatest significance of *Roots*. For many years now, increasingly large numbers of Americans have become fascinated trying to find where *they* came from. Genealogical societies in this country are hard-pressed to keep pace with the demand of Americans eager to learn of their personal heritage. Famous English genealogical societies, the kinds that construct family crests and keep track of Britain's nobility, now give their services to very middle-class Americans. Even the Boy Scouts have gotten into the picture, giving a merit badge for those boys who can trace a family history. It seems, the question on the lips of many Americans — a question symbolized by *Roots* — is "What is the heritage that *I* can claim?"

As a people, we're being driven back to the family picture album, and beyond, to learn our personal history. And at the heart of this migration into the past is the oldest of all quests — the search for identity. "Who am I?" seems to be the unspoken, ever-present question. "When all the facades are down, when the image I seek to project is removed, who am I? And where do I fit?" The book which came of Alex Haley's quest is so successful because it presents an archetype for our own self-understanding.

So does another book. The Bible, the best selling book of all times, is, also, a personal history book. You, undoubtedly, have heard the play on words "history" is actually "his story," and his story and his story — a story common to all. That's why we often read, in the Bible, words such as "Uzziah beget Jotham, and Jotham begat Ahaz, and Ahaz begat Hezekiah, and Hezekiah . . ." *We* fit in there, somewhere. "And Joe and Hazel begat Jim, and Jim and Dorothy begat Michelle," and so on down the line. The Bible is the story of God's creative participation in our lives, our history. It's our story.

The Old Testament lesson for today is very important. The story about God's call of Abraham is the beginning of the story of your family in faith and of mine. Here are our roots; this is our heritage and our identity.

Moses put this story in perspective. In speaking of Abraham and the patriarchs, Moses said, "A wandering Aramean was my father." Moses was establishing the roots of all God's people. "A wandering Aramean was my father" is an announcement of who we are — it locates us in the scope of history. You might say it's the Old Testament version of the Apostles' Creed — it defines us. As such, the statement reminds us of the divine promise received from our Lord.

The statement is also a confession. "My father was *only* an Aramean, a nomad unwelcomed anywhere but in the swamps and the barren desert, a gypsy quick to borrow the ideas (and the property) of others but with nothing much of value himself." This Old Testament creed places us solidly in the Divine's history of mankind, but it admits our place is not too attractive and not really praiseworthy.

If Alex Haley's story, *Roots,* has a drawback it's that it glorifies, out of proportion, the nobility and strength of its characters. Our common story and confession, as Christians, doesn't repeat this mistake. Arameans are dirty; Arameans are devious.

As an inheritor of an ancestry, it's important to know our common past is valuable. But it's also important to know it's not always beautiful. We should know we have the value of living in a long line of the faithful, but the ancestors of even the best of us seldom are something to brag about. Otherwise, we would think we are only pale successors and could never measure up to them.

In the wake of the televising of *Roots,* historian Kenneth Thomas published an account of the other side of the slavery story. He wrote a brief, factual history of a southern white family. It was a history of an English indentured servant of the early 1700's whose offspring became slave-owners. Some of the offspring were brawlers and shady owners of a carnival. Some were killers. Few were admirable. Yet, Thomas explains, this was the ancestry Jimmy Carter had to carry to the White House.

We are what our ancestors have left us to be. But, if that's all we are, then we're in sad shape. The painful truth is, although we have roots and they are valuable for our self-understanding, our roots usually are not very pretty. Many of our ancestors are worth little as models for us to imitate. That's even true of our religious ancestors.

Look at some of our ancestors in faith, those wandering Arameans we claim as fathers. They were more sinners than saints.

Abraham seemed forever clumsy. Once, while in Egypt, he tried to pass off his wife, Sarah, as his sister so a Pharaoh with a wandering eye would not become jealous and kill him to get her. The Pharaoh was insulted that Abraham would even think such a thing. Another time Abraham had to divide the land God had given him with his nephew Lot. Using the old formula of children, "I'll cut — you pick," Abraham allowed Lot to take the prime bottom land, while Abraham got only scrub brush. Frederick Buechner has said, "If a *schlemiel* is a person who goes through life spilling soup on people and a *schlemozzle* is the one it keeps getting spilled on, then Abraham was a *schlemozzle." (Peculiar Treasures,* p.3) Yet he's our family.

Then there's King David. We usually remember David for his battle against Goliath, his beautiful psalms, his mighty kingdom. But David was also a philanderer — he chased other men's wives. And when he caught them, as he did Bathsheba, he wasn't above knocking off the husband so he could marry the woman. Not exactly the ideal ancestor to imitate.

What about the prophet Elijah? Strong and brave, to be sure, but also a bit crude. The Bible says one day some city boys followed along behind the aging Prophet, calling him "Baldy." Elijah promptly summoned two she-bears who tore forty-two of the city boys limb from limb. He then continued on his way to keep an appointment at Mount Carmel. Our great-grandfather in faith, Elijah — are you sure you want to boast about him?

Then there's Jacob. With Abraham, Isaac, and Joseph, he is a Patriarch and at the very base of our family roots. What we often forget is Jacob's nickname was "tricky Jacob." He was sly and cunning. He cheated his brother out of their father's inheritance. He even ambushed one of God's angels in an effort to blackmail God to give him more blessings. By rights, his picture would never make it to the mantel in the family homestead. Yet he, too, is an ancestor in faith.

We are what our ancestors have left us to be: that's the message of the show *Roots*. But, we hope, there's more to us. We hope our story and our value as individuals doesn't come from merely adding a few more years of painful, aimless living to a common story; there's not much glory in adding one more gnarled limb to a sickly, scraggly family tree.

We *are* what our ancestors have left us to be. But that's not *all* we are. There's one more element to our heritage, at least our religious heritage. Our ancestors in faith left us not only a name, not only a histry, *but also a blessing* — God's blessing. "I will bless you," says the Lord to Abraham and his descendants, "and make your name great, so that you will be a blessing." What makes the heritage of the faithful, to which we belong, different from any other family tree and story the genealogists can dig up, is not that we're better than anyone else. Abraham, David, Elijah, and Jacob show we're no saints. What makes us different is we're blessed by God. God claims us. We are part of his *clan*. He *made* that investment in us; he established his kinship in Exodus when he said, "You will be my people, and I will be your God." And he demonstrated his involvement in our clan when he sent his Son to struggle and die on our behalf. It's not out of respect for our heritage God accepts us; it's out of involvement in our past that he loves us and stays involved in our present. It is why, in the Lord's Prayer, Christ permits us to say, "Our Father," when addressing God. This is a family affair.

"A wandering Aramean was my father." When we announce that, we remind ourselves we're part of a long line of the faithful, people who have been blessed by God. When we *confess* with those words, we remind ourselves we *need* this blessing of God.

Notice one other thing. This statement about our ancestors says more than our fathers in faith were dirty, devious Arameans. Our heritage is that of a *wandering* Aramean. We have no land, no property we can truly call our own. Abraham never did settle down in one place. Our life as God's children is a journey, always searching for a Promised Land where life is simple and good, but always enduring, in the meantime, the world we pass by — the confused world, the troubled world, the doubting world. And the irony is, it's not in that future land God promises to be with us, but in this present journey. It is the *wandering* Aramean who is our father and God child — not the settled, respectable, prosperous Aramean, but the searching one who was given God's blessing. In this life, we will never arrive at a Promised Land which, today, we see not so much as a place, but as a dreamed-of condition of wisdom, comfort, wealth, or security. This is the way God meant it to be. The creed of faith, which links us with our ancestors, never loses sight of the fact that the faithful are always wanderers, always pilgrims.

Even knowing our heritage doesn't give us security. We can't hide behind Abraham's robes. Indeed, the greatest irony here is, having roots, we are yet rootless. Having this heritage only reminds us we have no home. Examining our roots is not a nostalgia trip from which we can return to a comfortable secure present. It's a recognition that our present has no security in anything temporal. Wandering means lacking home, lacking many possessions, lacking even a country. As God's children, we inherit nothing except his blessing, his name, and his promise to be with us and help us make sense out of a senseless world.

Having roots in God's family means our roots cannot be in the world we see around us today. The starkness of that reality is demonstrated poignantly in a well-known movie of the 1960's — *Fiddler on the Roof*. As you may well know, this is a story of a village of Russian Jews. They're faithful Jews; they, too, can confess, "A wandering Aramean was my father." For them life was good; their village of Anatevka thrives and, in their prosperity, they see God's blessing. Then comes the pogrom, the government persecution. Now they must move on; they must lose their prosperity. But they manage to see that the blessing of God, greater than their prosperity, is the promise he made to them — the promise to be with them, to comfort them, to give direction to their wandering. At movie's end, these Jewish peasants pack their carts, singing mournfully of Anatevka, the abandoned home. But they conclude by sighing, "We'll find a new Anatevka; God will lead us. After all, he led our fathers!"

"A wandering Aramean was my father." When we announce and confess that, we *know* our roots and our identity. And we know we broken, but blessed, people are not rooted in a time or a place. We are rooted in a promise, in a faith, in a journey.

Exodus 17:3-7

He Can Quench All Your Thirsts

One of the funniest and wisest commentaries on human nature is the cartoon strip Hagar the Horrible. In one cartoon Hagar's son, Hamlet, asks his blank-faced father if he could help put his model ship in a bottle. Hagar frowns and proceeds to lecture the boy on how he should be more industrious in seeking solutions to his problems, how he should read and reason and not wait for the answers to his problems to be handed to him. Hamlet mumbles, "Thanks, Dad." Then, in the next room, he tells his mother, "Dad didn't know how, either."

Now in one sense, Hagar is right. Guidance and encouragement, when coupled with self-reliance, can often be more valuable than those easy solutions to our problems given to us by others. As the old saying puts it: "Give a hungry man a fish and you feed him for a day. Teach him how to fish and you feed him for a lifetime."

But in another sense, of course, Hagar failed miserably. His son had a need for something very specific and Hagar only gave him words. The boy may have been wiser and stronger for this encounter, but his boat remained outside the bottle.

Practical help vs. spiritual help — that's also an issue for those seeking God. It's an issue in the Bible. We see the contrast between the Old Testament lesson for this morning and our Gospel.

God, in the early books of the Bible, is very practical-minded. He does not hesitate to physically intervene in the life of his people. He plants a garden for Adam, his angels eat dinner with Abraham and wrestle with Jacob. He divides the Red Sea for Moses, crumbles the Jericho walls for Joshua, and gives Solomon wealth beyond his dreams. In today's First Lesson, the Israelites have just had their hunger assuaged by manna from heaven and flocks of tasty quail.

Now they complain they're thirsty. So Moses strikes a rock and out spurts a fountain to quench the thirst of all. When God told his covenant people he would watch over them he meant it in a practical, physical way. This Old Testament God is not above getting his hands dirty to help his people.

By contrast, look at our Gospel lesson. Jesus runs into a notorious sinner at a town well in Samaria. He is as thirsty as those Israelites with Moses but, in this story, it never says if he is given a drink. Instead, attention is on an invisible "living water" which will give this woman healing, strength, and peace. Jesus and the woman debate, inquire, forgive, inspire. But apparently they never drink. Whereas God's gift in the Exodus story is tangible and exactly what the Israelites requested, God's gift to the Samaritan woman is Jesus himself.

Does this mean God has shifted his focus in the world from practical help to "feeding the soul?" That's a common criticism by non-Christians who say the church is long on talk and short on action. Does God — and do his people — care more for theology and less for physical involvement with others? Certainly the New Testament deals extensively with teachings — the parables of Jesus, the Sermon on the Mount, the Pauline letters filled with advice. And certainly most churches today spend less money and energy offering practical help, such as soup kitchens or day care centers or clothing banks, than in giving such nontangibles as sermons, classes, and counseling. Is faithfulness, then, more a matter of sharing *living* water with the lost than H_2O with the thirsty?

Not according to the Bible. God's practical help and his spiritual nourishment are inseparably intertwined. In Exodus, God's gift of manna was also a gift of faith, since the manna could not be stored overnight and the people had to trust God would provide it anew each day. Only three chapters after giving water from the rock at Horeb, Yahweh quenches the people's thirst for permanent order and direction: he gives the Ten Commandments. The Promised Land they took over was not only fields and mountains and rivers; it was such intangibles as an identity, a confidence, and a sense of loving community.

God's practical and spiritual gifts are also inseparably intertwined in the Gospels. The purpose of Jesus' three-year ministry was proclamation of the coming divine kingdom, a "living water" kind of gift. Yet, it was the practical gift of his physical miracles — multiplying bread and fish for the hungry, healing the lame — that occupies almost two-thirds of the Gospel narrative and most attracted followers. In his day, his deeds spoke his love louder than his words.

In the Bible, God's words and deeds are inseparable. A story in Luke demonstrates this well. When a paralytic is brought to Jesus, our Lord sees the man's heart and his greatest needs and, therefore, offers words: "Your sins are forgiven." Then, both to address the man's other problem and, as Luke puts it, " 'that you may know that the Son of Man has authority on earth to forgive sins' — he said to the man who was paralyzed — 'I say to you, rise, take up your bed and go home.' And immediately he rose before them . . ." (Luke 5:24-25)

Throughout the Bible, God gave both practical and spiritual help without neglecting one in favor of the other. It's still true today. Some of God's gifts today are tangible and real. A young man and a young woman, both of whom are praying for the right person to marry, are brought together accidently. But it's no accident: it's the answer to prayer. So is the healing of an ill person in a way which perplexes the doctor. A hungry man on the church door step is given a grocery bag of food. The church secretary hands him the bag, but God is doing the giving.

Worldwide hunger and disease, discrimination and fear call for leaders to take concrete steps to show mercy and give justice. These persons step forward: Bishop Tutu, Mother Teresa, Martin Luther King, Jr., Dag Hammarskjold, Tom Dooley, Albert Schweitzer. The most famous humanitarians of our time have had a clear sense of being sent by God. God still gives streams of water to the parched. Just ask the farmers of northern Bangledesh where thousands of irrigation pumps have been installed because of your benevolence giving.

At the same time, the help most people seek from God today is a spiritual, invisible aid — courage before crisis, comfort in grieving, clarity in decision-making, forgiveness for a battle-scarred conscience. God gives this living water, too. And not only is God's help today both practical and spiritual, but the two natures of that help are still inseparably bound. How can a hungry person be given food without also finding acceptance, love, and hope? What troubled person, calmed and inspired by forgiveness or joy or hope, is not better able to use the resources God has given him?

Often the best way to find one kind of help is to look for the other. God best helps those people with a problem of the spirit, such as depression or loneliness, by prompting them to find a practical way to serve others. They make dinner for a neighbor just home from the hospital, volunteer to drive for Meals on Wheels, become a Big Brother or Big Sister to a parentless child. It's almost miraculous how helping others with their problems can make our own less painful and more manageable.

Likewise God's "living waters" can be far more tangible than just a spiritual lift. Get on your knees to ask for a right relationship with him and you may also find him giving healing for an illness, or a sudden job opening when you're unemployed and frantic with the search. God is not so heavenly minded that he's no earthly good.

One more thing. The inseparableness of God's practical and spiritual involvement in the world should remind us of how we are to act. There's more to living as his people than serving others. Our growth as Christians is stunted without a prayer and study and worship life. At the same time, calloused knees mean little without calloused hands.

Don't let your God be too small. And don't let yourself be too small. The waters he offers can quench every type of thirst we dare have.

When God Says "Go"

Several years ago Alvar Persson was elected mayor of Grove City, Minnesota. It was an unusual election, partly because of the size of the victory — Persson garnered eighty percent of the vote — partly because Persson is a Lutheran minister and not a politician, but mostly because Persson wasn't even running for office. No one was. Next to the word *Mayor* on the ballot was a blank space. Only write-in votes could be cast. Of the eleven people whose names were written in, Persson was the clear choice — 202 votes of the 255 cast.

After the election, Persson was asked his reaction. He could only say: "I'm touched by this honor. But I didn't ask for it. Why pick me?"

Why indeed? As a minister, Persson should have been used to being led to his job by an irresistible force. The call to the ministry, like an election by write-in votes, is unpredictable, illogical, and almost impossible to turn down. Like a write-in vote, it's flattering, but also flooring. That goes for the lay ministry such as yours, the ministry of sharing God's love and God's Word with your neighbors, as well as for the ordained ministry. Few long-standing Christians are faithful because they coldly and calmly calculated the benefits to them. Rather, we're much like John Kennedy, when someone asked him what led him to be a war hero. "It was entirely involuntary" he said. "Someone sank my boat!"

Becoming Christians was involuntary for most of us, too. Most of us were grabbed —

By another Christian's love that wouldn't let go;

By turmoil of the soul which was calmed by faith;

By a vision of what God's people can do with the world.

God seldom asks for volunteers. He selects the unexpecting to be his people.

One day, 3000 years ago, the prophet Samuel came to the Judean house of Jesse, a pillar of the community. God had told Samuel he would find a new king for Israel among Jesse's sons. The prophet found many eager candidates — seven *All-American* men (or should I say All-Israelite men) each in the prime of life, three of them soldiers. But God inspired Samuel to turn down all of them. Then, with a Cinderella twist, the youngest child of the family is summoned from the fields where he is watching the sheep. An amazed little David is annointed the next king.

God chooses us more than we choose him. In some, he puts a hunger for something — inner peace, perhaps, or a purpose to living. It's a hunger assuaged only when we surrender to a life of faithfully serving him. "Our hearts are restless," Augustine said, "until they rest in thee."

For others, the choice is seemingly accidental. No one else was willing to be bishop of late fourth century Milan, so a stunned layman named Ambrose is tabbed and becomes a famous saint in the process. When a teacher fails to show up for Sunday school one week, you're pressed into service; a generation later, you're still teaching. What the world calls an accident, the faithful call God's providence. Not only does God do the calling, but he calls the least likely of us. Samuel annointed the runt of Jesse's family as king. And even Samuel could not envision this shepherd boy killing Goliath a short time later.

It's a numbing thought, being God's elect. Like Alvar Persson, I suspect we're tempted to say, "I'm touched by this honor. But I didn't want it. Why pick me?" Then we add our excuses:

"I don't speak well — how can I talk to my neighbor about God?"

"I'm guilty of so many sins — how can I be an example of Christian living?"

"I don't feel spiritual —- how can I contribute meaningfully to a Sunday worship?"
God has heard such apologies before.

From Moses: "I cannot speak for you; I am slow of speech and of tongue."

From young Jeremiah: "I cannot speak for thee, Lord God, I am just a child."

From Jonah the missionary: "I cannot represent God — I don't understand his merciful ways."

From the centurion, whose servant Jesus healed: "I am not worthy that Christ should come under my roof."

From Simon Peter: "Depart from me, Christ, for I am a sinful man."

In each case, God refused to accept their excuse. He insisted he wanted them, flaws and all.

Oh, occasionally God does choose the religiously "tall, dark, and handsome" figure. But the results seldom are gratifying. King Saul was such a figure. Saul was chosen king because he had everything — courage, size, skill as a warrior, good looks. But this obvious choice soon turned sour. He became selfish, ruthless, and later went mad.

What about Matthias, the man chosen in Acts to replace Judas as a disciple? Apparently, the other disciples elected him because he looked like a natural-born leader. But, after his election, the Bible never mentions him again.

God occasionally makes the obvious choice in choosing his servants. But only occasionally. Usually, he chooses people who are full of doubt, not overly bright, cantankerous, humble (and have good reason to be humble.) Usually, he chooses people just like us. That's the secret of the success of our religion. Little people, common people, witnessing to a most uncommon faith, intriguing all who listen, by claiming that a man executed as a criminal makes all the difference in their lives. It's not the charm of the messenger which makes our faith attractive — it's the beauty of the message. David, Peter, Isaiah, Abraham — they were no supermen. And neither need we be.

The secret of our election as God's servants in the world is this — God chooses us, not because of what we can do for him, but because of what he can do *with* us. Our availability interests God more than our ability.

Look at the disciples. The New Testament suggests they were neither brighter nor nicer than other people. They continually missed the point, always jockeyed for position and, when the chips were down, were interested only in saving their own skins. Their sole qualification seems to have been their initial willingness to rise to their feet when Jesus said "Follow me." But God used those twelve backwoodsmen to transform the world. As St. Paul put it later, "God chose what is foolish in the world to shame the wise;

God chose what is weak in the world to shame the strong.''

When God chooses us to hold up his Word to the world, he tells us we don't need to be anything other than ourselves. We need not pretend to be someone great.

A well-known *Peanuts* cartoon makes that point in a backwards way. Lucy spots her brother Linus as he shoots an imaginary arrow from an imaginary bow. She says to Charlie Brown beside her: "Good grief, now he's Robin Hood. If he sees a movie about skin diving, he plays skin diver for a week. If he sees a cowboy movie, we hear nothing but shooting. If he sees a movie about mountain climbing, then he's crawling up all the furniture." Charlie Brown thinks a moment, then asks: "Why don't you take him to a movie about Albert Schweitzer?"

The grace in our commission to be God's servants is we don't have to try to be someone we aren't. No uniforms, no badges, no special tools are needed. Only some knowledge of his Word and an eagerness to live it and share it with others.

But although God doesn't ask us to be someone other than ourselves, he does make us more than ourselves. As servants of God, we're no longer just Phyllis or George or Sally. Now we're his messengers, empowered by his spirit, working for his kingdom. The priesthood of all believers is how Luther put it. When God sends us as his representatives, we enter into a partnership with him. We needn't be self-conscious and afraid of that responsibility, as were Moses, Isaiah, and the rest. In this partnership, our Lord is the senior member. It's his Word, and not our words, which bears the burden of proof. That's why God can afford to choose, as his servants, fishermen and shepherds, truck drivers and homemakers.

When God chooses people to be his servants, he chooses common people. When he commands his servants to go into the world, they go; with questions sometimes, or fear or a lack of foresight, but they go. And God sees them through.

And what is the task of God's servants? What are we called to do? It varies from person to person.

"Govern my nation," he told David.

"Free my people," he commanded Moses.

"Feed my sheep," he told Peter.

"Preach my Word," he ordered Paul.

The ministry to which God calls you is as unique as you are yourself: visiting the ill, perhaps, or singing in the choir; building cathedrals or sweeping them out; knocking on doors or teaching Sunday school. The nature of your ministry is for you and God to work out, in prayer and trial.

Only remember this — it will be a ministry of service. Even as king, David's chief concern was the welfare of others and the glorification of God. More than a ministry of service, it will be a ministry which no one else can do in your place. God summons us to be workers, not spectators. This is a priesthood of *all* believers.

When God says, "Go as my servant into the world," he is speaking to each of us. And he expects us to obey. It's our comfort to know he will be with us, and the rewards of fullness of living far outweigh the burdens and the risks. When we know this, then we know the task is not too great. And, with David and Peter and all the rest, we can say, "I will go; send me."

A Daffy, Magnificent Hope

They still tell the story at William and Mary College of daffy, magnificent President Ewell. For a century and a half, this prestigious Virginia school had been a leader among American universities. Then came the Civil War. In the hard days of Reconstruction which followed, William and Mary went bankrupt. Soon it had a deserted campus, decaying buildings, and no students. As with so many Southern schools, after that tragic war, it was written off as dead by everyone.

Everyone, except its president. He had given his best years to advancing the liberal arts through that school. He refused to give up now. So, every morning, President Ewell went to the deserted campus, climbed the tower of its main building, and rang the bells, calling the school to class. He acted as if the school was still there. People thought he was crazy. But for seven years, every day, President Ewell rang the bells at William and Mary, in defiance of the despair and hopelessness that would destroy everything he held valuable. And eventually, miraculously, it worked. Others caught his vision. Students, teachers, and *money* returned. Today, America's second oldest university thrives again, because of the hope of a daffy, magnificent dreamer.

Ezekiel was made from the same stuff as President Ewell, but with vinegar added to his blood. This Old Testament prophet saw God in a fiery chariot and spoke of Jerusalem as a rusty pot that boiled its citizens. He ate scrolls and burned his hair to shock people into paying attention. But there was a method to his madness. For Ezekiel, also, was doggedly hopeful. He had two missions in life — to warn Israel of God's displeasure with her disregard of him and then, after she suffered his wrath and sat stewing in exile, to offer the promise that he would save her.

In our First Lesson, Ezekiel, in a vision, is led by God to a valley of dry bones, a symbol for Israel in exile. God tells Ezekiel to prophesy to these bones, "Behold, I will cause breath to enter you, and you shall live. And I shall lay sinews upon you, and will cause flesh to come upon you, and cover you with skin, and put breath in you, and you shall live; and you shall know that I am the Lord." Sure enough, as Ezekiel spoke, the bones became living people.

The vision of the valley of dry bones was Ezekiel's summons to hope. These bones were Israel, broken as a nation, scattered throughout the land of exile, fossil-dry in soul. Only a divinely-inspired vision could see them coming together as skeletons, then people, then a nation. Only a daffy, magnificent vision.

Today we live in a reasoned age where such daring hope is written off as fantasy. Christianity is not so much hamstrung by little hope as by little hopes. Petty, no-risk hopes too easily become our stock in trade. We hope it doesn't rain on the church picnic, that Sunday's offering can match Monday's bills, that the plastic-faced couple sitting behind us will hold their marriage together for the children's sake. We're taught to be practical and productive — level-headed achievers. This means setting our sights only on targets we know we can hit.

How different were God's people in the Bible! Those children of God who hoped for the most were rewarded the most. Abraham set off across the desert for a Promised Land, sustained only by the wild promise from God that his descendants would be as numerous as the stars. Today one and one-half billion people claim him as their father in faith. Ezekiel asserted that Israel could rise from its living grave as captives and return to its own land. Within a generation it was done and Judiasm was born. In the Gospels, countless blind, diseased, lame, and grieving people came to Jesus with pained longing in their eyes. Jesus never failed to heal them.

The leaders of God's church more recently were just as expansive in their hopes. Luther gave birth to a greatly revitalized church because he sought a purified one. The Pilgrims founded a Christian land because they envisioned a free "nation under God." Today integration and racial harmony are expected in America because Martin Luther King, Jr. and others dared to say "I have a dream." Daffy and magnificent dreams? Perhaps. But successful, too.

Our world craves open-hearted people who dare to dream big.

Two superpowers clutching enough nuclear weapons to destroy the world eight times over glare at each other, and no one knows how to disarm. The elderly and the unemployed — many of them members of this church — stare at the dropping temperatures and no one knows how they can pay for fuel. Seven million refugees of famine sit huddled in relief camps in Africa and no one knows how many can be saved by our help.

In only one place can solutions be born — in hope. No amount of work, indeed, of prayer, can change the world or our lives unless we can conceive of that change. Hope is a conception of what might be.

Theologian Frederick Buechner, in an article on Hope, writes, "Christianity is mainly wishful thinking. Even the part about judgment and Hell reflects the wish that somewhere the score is being kept. Sometimes wishing is the wings the truth comes true on." In other words, if you can't dream it, you can't have it. But if you dare to dream, perhaps . . . just perhaps.

Such hope is more than idle daydreaming. It is a life-giving power as real as the invisible energy from the electrical outlet on the wall. Karl Menninger tells about a group of doctors who survived the horrors of slave labor in a World War II concentration camp. Each night they secretly came together and shared their knowledge in a small medical society. They believed someday what they were learning and sharing would be of benefit to the world. While scores of other prisoners around them died every week, almost all of the doctors lived. As Menninger put it, "They were kept alive by hope."

Is it any wonder the most lively committees and organizations of the church are those which have developed a goal, a vision of the future, and are eagerly working toward it?

A vision of the future, what we call hope, is the greatest animating force we know. Notice, though, to be realistic, hope must trust in a power greater than the problem it faces. Hope must be grounded in someone or something, lest we become like King Canute, futilely commanding the ocean tide to stop. For many problems of the world, there is only one power great enough to encourage hope. That's why Ezekiel was quick to envision God breathing on those dry bones bringing them alive. No one else could perform such a miracle. This kind of hope is more than just wishful thinking. It is the absolute confidence the future will be good because the future is God's.

Some time ago, an adult Sunday school class was discussing heaven. The question was raised, "Are Christians so greatly concerned with eternal life that we're insensitive to the world's needs and the human possibilities in this life?" "So heavenly-minded that we're no earthly good" is the familiar phrase. After some thoughtful discussion, the people present said, "No — hope for the future in the next life *is not* a form of escapism from this one." History confirms that. The Christians who did most for the present world were those who thought most of the next. The apostles, who set on foot the humanizing and conversion of the Roman Empire, the great men and women who kept civilization alive in the Middle Ages, the reformers who promoted the Renaissance, the English evangelicals who abolished the slave trade in Europe — they all improved this life precisely because they were so concerned with the next one. As C.S. Lewis has said, "It is since Christians have largely ceased to think of the other world that we are so ineffective in this one. Aim at Heaven and you will get Earth 'thrown in'; aim at Earth and you will get neither."

To have high hopes is not to dream the impossible dream. With God, all things are possible, said St. Paul. The whole point of the resurrection was God could take the worst possible fate — betrayal, shame, painful execution — and turn it into victory. In fact, the Christian realists are those who *do* dream, think big, have high hopes for what God can do. They've seen the inspiring power of the resurrection. It's those who refuse to dream who are out of touch with reality. As Christians, we believe in a fourth dimension — beyond what we can see and touch is a God invisibly active among us. Don't count him out simply because you can't recognize him or understand him. He hasn't counted you out.

Martin Luther, in later life, suffered periods of depression when he thought so often of his problems that he forgot God's promises. One day he seemed especially gloomy, so his wife, Katie, dressed herself in black mourning clothes. When Luther demanded to know why she was in mourning, she said, "I thought God died." Luther got the message.

One other thing. After hope has led you to pray fervently and to place the problem in God's hands, except the unexpected. God will never forget us, but usually he will surprise us. When Ezekiel told his people God would "raise you from your graves," a return from exile was all he conceived. Today we see these as words prophetic of the resurrection.

When God first told young Abraham he would be the father of nations, God never mentioned Abraham would have to wait until he was over 100 years old to have a son. When King Solomon prayed to God for wisdom to rule, instead of wealth, a delighted God gave him both. When downtrodden Israel, under the Romans, prayed for a Messiah to save them, no one dreamed he would be born in a stable in Bethlehem and his salvation would extend to the next life. God will never forsake our open-hearted hopes, but he seldom will give us exactly what we expect. Usually his gifts are grander but less recognizable than we ever imagined.

We hope for a cure for an illness but, instead, uncover untapped reserves of strength, love, and wisdom for dealing with it. We hope for adequate rains and a big harvest to end a famine but, instead, are overwhelmed by donations to help the victims. We hope for happiness through a comfortable lifestyle but, instead, find joy in simple living. One couple I know was unnerved after they prayed that their daughter find a Christian roommate. A month later she announced she was engaged to be married!

It's magnificently daffy, this hope. It dares believe an unseen God will enter our lives and influence our future. For countless Christians, though, it's the only thing that has pulled them through the pits of despair back into the light of God's blessings. You say hope in God's providence is an impossible dream in this dirty world? You're right. But only the dreams that are impossible are sure, for they belong to God.

Isaiah 50:4-9a   *Passion (Palm) Sunday*

Christ's Passion Portraits

The task before us that afternoon was simple enough. The newly remodeled church lounge had a wall which needed a picture; everyone agreed it should be a portrait of Christ. The question was — what should Jesus look like? Five hundred years before Christ's birth, Isaiah had predicted he would have "no form or comeliness that we should look at him, and no beauty that we should desire him." Except for the unnerving remark, the Bible never mentions Jesus' appearance. So, which of the scores of paintings available should we choose?

Everyone had a favorite. The youth representative to the committee had torn from a catalog a picture of a laughing Jesus. "It's a fresh look," he said. "It makes Jesus the kind of person it would be fun to know." An elderly housewife held up a copy of Sallman's famous *Head of Christ* with its glowing, calm face and its placid eyes staring off into space. She would gladly donate this from her bedroom wall. The Sunday school teacher suggested a scene of Jesus kissing a child in his arms — she once had seen the picture on a bookmark. The psychologist wanted the portrait of a tousled-haired Christ staring out intently and expectantly. His eyes would seem to follow you anywhere in the room.

It wasn't surprising that our preferences were so predictable. "God made man in his own image," a theological wag once observed, "and ever since we have tried to repay the compliment." A great goal of the Christian life has always been to be "Christlike." So we try to mold our personalities, our attitudes, our actions in imitation of him. Or maybe we simply admire the image of Christ most congenial to our own personalities. No wonder I'm perplexed, deciding which of the attractive images of Christ offered by painters and preachers is most accurate. But I'm also concerned knowing we can never measure up to *one* of those images, let alone *all*.

Still, we try. Ever since the faithful of St. Paul's Antioch were first derisively called Christians, which literally means "little Christs," we've tried to be just that — wise and warm, strong and loving.

But what of the darker side of Christ? The Lord we see in these tragic days of Holy Week is one few want to imitate. He is the Lord of suffering and pain. On this day, he is painted slouched on a too-short donkey, riding quietly through the happy tumult to his doom. Later he's portrayed kneeling, small and afraid, in the dark Garden of Gethsemane. After that, it's with a bramble of thorns, twisted in a circle, tearing his scalp.

If we are to be little Christs, it is important we also imitate this "man of sorrow, acquainted with grief," and not treat him "as one from whom men hide their faces." (Isaiah 53:3) Otherwise, he becomes a mere caricature of a nice guy. He becomes a Hollywood image, surface deep.

The passion portrait of Christ is the man of integrity. Isaiah puts these words in Christ's mind as the Son of God rides into Jerusalem on Palm Sunday, "I have set my face like a flint." (Isaiah 50:7) Imagine this painting of Christ — iron-jawed, chiseled features, eyes that ignore the cheering crowds lining the road as they stare rigidly ahead at a goal only they can see. This face like a flint cannot be chipped away by convenient compromise with entrenched evil. And it cannot be scratched by jealous critics. It's hard to love a face like a flint. But, respect for it comes naturally, the kind of respect not generated by the popular portraits of Christ.

This Palm Sunday was a dangerous day for Christ. He had withstood the temptation of Satan in the Wilderness, now he had to ignore almost identical temptations shouted from hundreds of adoring voices — power, honor, love, if only he would consent to be their king. But they were too late. He had given himself completely into the plans of the Father. It was this pledge which compelled him to ride on to a frightful providence he could only vaguely suspect. It's not that he didn't know the people and problems swirling around him.

He knew the crowds were fickle and could turn on him if he did not please them.

He knew the religious leaders were jealous and executed reformers. He knew some people would sell their souls for thirty pieces of silver. He knew even friends can desert you through neglect or fear. Christ knew the danger of that ride.

However he knew something to be even more important. He knew he had to keep a covenant with the Father, he had to follow conscience rather than opportunity. In a world which believes the only success is success, Jesus was rewriting the rules. Sacrifice, submission, and service would be his credo. In the meantime, he rode on with a face like a flint. Integrity demanded no less.

The passion portrait of Christ is the man of righteous anger. Soon after entering Jerusalem, on this day, Christ went to the temple and drove out the corrupt money-changers. In this painting of Christ, he would be speaking with a whip, robes billowing from his thrusts, rage streaking his face. He's overturning tables and pouring out money and shouting at the stunned bankers. This painting could be captioned with the Psalmist's words, "Zeal for thy house will consume me." (Psalm 69:9) A zeal for justice erupts in righteous anger.

We call the last days of Christ his passion. The old meaning of this word is suffering and, certainly, our Lord knew that kind of passion during his trial, beatings, and crucifixion.

But the dictionary says passion also means intense emotional drive or excitement. And our Lord knew that kind of passion, too. He was not a one-dimensional figure, the way the popular paintings imply — you know the paintings, where he's quietly holding a lamb, quietly knocking on a door, quietly gazing into space or quietly walking to Emmaus with two followers. Any red-letter edition of the Bible — which records Christ's words in red — will show our Lord was never that quiet.

Rather, he was a dynamic man. He mentally and emotionally wrestled with the devil for forty days in the wilderness. In debate, he cleverly threw parables and trick questions at the Pharisees, who had tried to trip him up with their own clever questions. And Jesus threw anger at them, too. He called them snakes and broods of vipers and growled, "You are like tombs covered with white-wash — nice looking on the outside but inside full of dead bones and filth."

Remember how the Bible often said Jesus sighed? That's a mistranslation of the word sigh. The original Greek word does not indicate grief; it signifies indignation. Jesus was angry — angry at corruption and angry at people's selfish refusal to recognize the coming Kingdom of God. It's his eagerness to usher in that King-dom of God — not some placid emotional exterior — that is the only constant in the nature of Jesus. He was not "gentle Jesus meek and mild," as the nineteenth century portrayed him. That misun-derstands his teachings of "turn the other cheek" and love and toler-ance, which were not founded on mildness but motivated by the total irrelevance of worldly concern, in the face of the overriding need to prepare for God's Kingdom. In turning the other cheek, he was sim-ply turning away from playing the world's games.

In the words of theologian Michael Grant, Jesus "was a stormy personage with a mighty vein of granite in His character." *(Jesus: An Historian's Review of the Gospels,* p. 76) If we want a picture of Jesus we can emulate, let it be set here in the temple with our Lord consumed by zeal. Paul claimed Christ came to our world "to purify for himself a people of his own who are *zealous* for good deeds." (Titus 2:14) Our world desperately needs such zeal. We, too, readily, wink at corruption and yawn at the arms race and glance away from the gaunt faces of hunger staring out from the T.V. news. We, too eagerly, admire people who are "laid back" — which sim-ply means they're keeping a comfortable distance from life — and when we leave each other we, too mindlessly, toss the phrase "take it easy." Once we cared enough to say, "Goodbye," which was short for "God bless." Now the blessing we need is zeal.

The passion portrait of Christ can be the flint-faced man of in-tegrity or the scowling man of righteous anger. It can also be the haunting portrait of the lonely man.

The classic painting by Hoffman of Christ kneeling in the Garden of Gethsemane shows him small and huddled, engulfed by the night's blackness. That fits his mood. It was agony waiting for Judas and his arrestors, agony wondering if he had missed God's plan for vic-tory at some fork in the road, agony thinking of the coming pain. But at least he wasn't hiding. He wasn't on the road to safe Galilee or back in the upper room drowning his fear in wine. He knew lone-liness like this cannot be escaped. Loneliness haunts everyone — the loneliness of being single and aching to share your life and your love; the loneliness of being married to the one you love and yet having no words more than surface deep; the loneliness of being sur-rounded by laughing, warm people and none of them knows your name; the loneliness of following conscience when others are op-portunists; the loneliness of a dead-end job, of a secret sin, of es-trangement. Christ knew such loneliness is inevitable in life.

the loneliness of following conscience when others are opportunists; the loneliness of a dead-end job, of a secret sin, of estrangement. Christ knew such loneliness is inevitable in life.

But he also knew he could deal with it constructively. That's why he went to the Garden and put himself in the Father's hands through prayer. Long before we ask, God is ready to comfort and strengthen.

Christ knew loneliness can be dealt with. That's why he brought James and John and Peter with him. He was able to share his loneliness, to tell his friends of his fear, and ask them for support. Although they kept falling asleep, Jesus returned to them frequently to unburden himself and to talk. The command to love is the command to share loneliness and, in that sharing, to find the community and the intimacy which erases it.

A cherished foe, this loneliness, even a divine gift not to be ashamed of or avoided. Without it, we would never hunger for love with others and intimacy with God.

In the Garden, the fear and the heartache of loneliness drove Christ to his knees. But that's not a bad place to be.

They're stark pictures of Christ, these passion portraits of the man of integrity, the man of zeal, the lonely man. They're stark and they're intimidating for those who see them as a model for our lives. But the Holy Week drama reminds us there are dark expanses of life which cannot be faced by smiles or the spirit of "gentle Jesus, meek and mild." Having more than one dimension allowed our Lord to respond to all the coming week could throw at him. Having more than one dimension does no less for us "little Christs."

Ecclesiastes said it best. "For everything there is a season . . . a time to break down and a time to build up; a time to weep and a time to laugh; a time to mourn, and a time to dance; a time to keep silence, and a time to speak."

Our comfort is knowing that faithfulness takes many faces.

Our challenge is finding the season for each.

"If Only . . . "

It never should have happened to a good Jewish man. At sundown, the beginning of this day as the Jews reckon it, he gathers with his friends for the holy meal of Passover, an act quite pious and proper. By the end of this day, at tomorrow's sundown, he's dead, executed as a traitor. If he really was faithful to his religion and innocent of crime, as even Pilate admitted, how could he be tried and found guilty? And if he really was God's Son, the Messiah, as his disciples claimed, how could he die, as a criminal? It's no wonder the gawkers who stand at the cross beat their breasts. Confusion reigned! The world turned upside down!

On this Passover evening before his death, life seemed so rational and so reassuring. God was on their side, these people of Jerusalem. He always had been. He would never desert them. As the disciples gathered at the Passover dinner table, so did hundreds of families throughout Jerusalem. They gathered to recall God's actions at the time of Moses: how God stepped into human history, rearranged the events of man, crippled the Egyptians with plagues and death, and how he patiently succored and guided the Israelites into nationhood. That's the kind of God these Jews had stacked their faith upon, a God able and willing to transform history to his own purpose.

But where was their God on Friday? His chosen people, making a mockery of their Torah; his divine representative, stretched across an executioner's rack. God seemed absent. His people reached that brink of disaster they had known so many times before. But this time they went over that brink. No last minute reprieve, no sudden miracle shattering the cross. The God accustomed to intervening in history, transforming history, now was allowing history to run its own disastrous course.

For the disciples, on this night, it was unthinkable God would fail to aid his penitent people. In the Passover meal each family not only recalled how God delivered his people from destruction, they attempted to re-experience the scene in Egypt 1200 years before. And, in that reenactment, they found anew their identity as God's chosen people.

In the upper room the disciples, with their food, recalled how God had spared their ancestors. The unleavened bread, baked before it had time to rise, reminded them of the haste with which their ancestors left the land of Pharaoh. The radishes and bitter herbs reminded them of the harsh life of Egypt from which God had delivered them. And the roasted lamb reminded them of the unblemished paschal lambs, sacrificed so their blood might be sprinkled on the Hebrew's doors in Egypt; God's avenging angel of death would see the blood stain and pass over in search of Egyptian victims. None of the disciples in the upper room dreamed their leader and host would soon be their new paschal lamb. How could they think that? They celebrated a God who saved his favorite people, not sacrificed them.

Even more important to their remembering than the foods of Passover were the words of Passover. At this meal, the Jews always had recounted the Haggadah, the tale refined into the poetry of a traditional chant:

If God had only freed us in Egypt to let us drown in the sea,
it would have been enough —
but he permitted us to cross on dry land.
If God had only brought us to the desert to let us die of hunger,
it would have been enough —
but he fed us with manna.
If God had only fed us with manna to let us wander aimlessly
in the desert,
it would have been enough —
but he brought us to Mt. Sinai.

Verse after verse, God's decisive intervention was recounted at the Passover meal. Few thought of the disaster of the next day.

If God had only given us the Torah to sustain us in the wilderness,
it would have been enough —
but he led us into the land of Israel.

Verse after verse, each speaking of a God who plucks his people out of the jaws of destruction.

But, by this coming afternoon of the cross, that God seemed absent. The ground shook, the temple curtain split, night's darkness came before its time. No God intervened to transform the disaster.

And yet, God *was* there. Unknown to anyone for days, unknown by most for centuries, God had not abandoned his people. He was there in their history, but this time as one willing to endure history, rather than one who transforms it. God was there, stretched out on a cross.

The script of history was rewritten that day. No longer would God's love be shown only through the blessings he gives his people. Henceforth that love also would be known through the sufferings he can share with us. In every Auschwitz, in every dank hold of a slave ship, in every urban slum, in every dark, lonely night God can now dare to be present, because he was willing to suffer the ultimate on the cross. To show that nothing is greater than his love for us, God wrote this chapter of our common history in blood — his own blood.

The script of history was rewritten that day. But the form need not change. The Passover's Haggadah poem can simply add a new verse. "If God had only shown that he was not above suffering death in the ugliest part of our history it would have been enough . . ." The end of the verse, words about defeating death and rising from the grave would not be known for several days. For the moment, only his flesh, limp upon the cross, is before us. "If God had only shown his love by sacrificing his Son for us, it would have been enough . . . " On this day, it is enough.

They Crucified Our Lord

They crucified our Lord.
Our crosses today are silver and gold,
antiseptic and shiny,
a symbol of triumph.
Not so on that day.

The cross was the ultimate execution rack. It's purpose was simple — to bring as much pain and as much shame as possible upon the victim — and upon each witness.

Could you bear to be a witness?

They made him walk through Jerusalem's main streets, carrying the cross-beam of the cross. His face streamed blood from the twisted bramble of thorns jammed on his head and tearing his scalp. A crown they called it, all the more to mock him. Bent by the weight of this timber, he looks like no king, "his appearance was so marred, beyond human semblance."

As he stumbles up the steep streets, a soldier marches before him announcing his crime to the merchants and shoppers. At the execution site, he is stripped of all his clothing — not all except his loin cloth, as painters down through the ages have modestly portrayed — but *all* his clothing. Then he is hung before his mother and friends. "He had no form or comeliness that we should look at him." Could you witness such shame?

He's there as a pawn sacrificed in the game of politics. The Roman governor knows his death is unjust, but he knows, too, this execution is expedient to placate the masses. Sentence passed, the governor turned his back, washed his hands, and our Lord was led away "despised and rejected by men . . . as one from whom men hide their faces."

He's there, too, because his supporters have deserted him. In fear, they "all like sheep have gone astray; each have turned every one to his own way." The loneliness is as galling as the shame and rejection.

At the top of Golgotha, the hill hideously resembling a skull, they force him to lay on the cross. His arms are tied to it with ropes. The flesh of his hands is torn open as the nails split the muscles and crack and dislodge the bones. As the cross is hoisted in place, the weight pulling on the spikes in the hands makes the pain even worse. The feet are put together — the spike is driven through and crushes them. Finally the cross is erect and he is "exalted and lifted up, and . . . very high." But could you witness such a sight?

A famous painting by Sigismund Goetzke suggests we cannot bear to witness this sight, or at least we will not witness it. Entitled "Despised and Rejected," it has, at its center, our suffering Lord nailed to the Roman altar, with an angel hovering above, holding the Gethsemane cup. Around him is a panorama of humanity. Yet, none of these people look at the cross. The scientist stares at his test tube and the sports addict his sports page. The society doll plays with her flowers coyly, aware of the admiring gaze of a fashionable young man. The politician has his crowd, the ditch digger his beer, the artist his cigarette. At the foot of the cross, a woman in rags, with a baby, sits dejected; in her despair, even she does not look up. In the distance, a widow with her lonely burden of grief stares only at the ground. Alone on the cross, our Lord is "cut off out of the land of the living." The world, engrossed in its own pursuits — its business, pleasures, gain, games, and grief — has no time for, and no thought of, Christ, who is still "despised and rejected of men." Or is it these people dare not look at the cross, so upsetting is the sight?

On the cross, the physical pain was so great the victims always were drugged. But Jesus refuses the pain-killing wine mingled with myrrh. He wishes to remain alert, and stoically endures. "He was oppressed, and he was afflicted, yet he opened not his mouth." So the cross takes its full toll.

Could you bear to witness as blood oozes out of the wounds festering in the mid-eastern sun?

As the flies swarm about the open flesh and into the unprotected eyes, mouth, and nose?

As the cross is stained and the ground, at its foot, puddled by vomit and body wastes?

A medical analysis of death on the cross leaves little to the imagination. Crucifixion resulted in severe pain because the body was hanging on nails through the wrists. The muscles extending from chest to arm were stretched and nearly stopped the ability to breathe, as they held the chest expanded. Little oxygen reached the muscles, which led to spasms and severed tendons. To relieve the pain in the arms, hands, and chest, the victim would try to push himself up using the nails through his feet as a brace. Within minutes, the pain in his feet would be unbearable. The body would sag. Then the process would begin once more, each time more feebly than the last. Gasping for air, the victim "poured out his soul to death."

Death comes from lack of breath and loss of blood.

It comes from exposure to the sun and the wind.

It comes from the attacks of the vultures and wild dogs that wait nearby, hungry.

Sometimes, death comes from going mad.

They crucified our Lord. Could you bear to be a witness?

God Is No Respecter Of Persons

Do you like trivia questions? Try these:

In what country of the world are the most Bic pens sold per capita? What has replaced the 44 revolver as the Great Equalizer in the West? What unique design appears on Sears, Roebuck's best-selling women's shirts?

The answers: Bic pens are most popular in Zaire. In that African country, however, people don't write with most of the Bic pens — they wear them. Any man who can scrape together an extra $2.00 will buy a half dozen pens and stick them all in his shirt pocket. It's a status symbol, a symbol that he can read and write, even if he can't; and that he has a white-collar job, even if he doesn't.

Western outfitters report that ordinary men who 100 years ago would have worn a gun so others might think of them as more than ordinary, are today wearing high-heeled cowboy boots. It seems an extra three inches will do wonders for one's ego.

At Sears, the best-selling woman's shirt bears the autograph of Cheryl Tiegs. It outsells shirts without her autograph four to one. Women seem to think some of the popular model's beauty and charisma will rub off on them if they identify with her.

Trivia questions. And yet, not trivial. At the heart of all these facts, stands a stark reality — people are hungry for status. From Zaire to Sears, people want to be looked-up-to. Indeed, psychologists today tell us the most basic human drive is not sexual, as Freud thought, nor for power, as Jung thought — it's the drive for respect. We'll do almost anything to be admired, because admiration gives us worth.

That's the reason our First Lesson today is so unnerving. St. Peter's statement to the Roman, Cornelius, we quoted from the

Revised Standard Version of the Bible — "Truly, I perceive that God shows no partiality, but in every nation any one who fears him and does what is right is acceptable to him." The King James Version puts that first line more graphically — "Truly I perceive that God is no respecter of persons."

Imagine that! What we seek above all else means nothing to our Lord. God doesn't give people respect. Even the best of us don't win his admiring eye. Our success doesn't impress him — he's no respecter of persons.

How hard it must have been for Peter to accept that. Peter had been a great respecter of persons. He had always been a true-blue Jew, for whom faithfulness to the God of Abraham was the only real measure of a person's worth. Even after three years with open-hearted Jesus, this devout Galilean could not forget, in his own words to Cornelius, "how unlawful it is for a Jew to associate with or to visit any one of another nation." So it's remarkable God would send pious Peter to minister to this pagan soldier.

Yet, those last days of Christ showed that even Peter, the best and the brightest of God's chosen people, wasn't good enough to gain God's respect. Peter deserted Jesus, cursed and hid. Could it be if Christ's forgiveness of Peter, on Easter, did not return the disciple's pride, at least it did give him a heart sensitive for the shortcomings of others? Could it be this same humiliated saint was the perfect choice to tell the foreigner of God's grace?

God is no respecter of persons — he is not partial to one race over another, once class over another, one nation over another. Our human accomplishments and abilities simply are not very impressive to the Almighty.

If God doesn't show us the same respect others do, it may be because he remembers better than we, the source of our beauty and brains, our talent and treasures. Like a child on Christmas night, who hoards from his siblings the toys he was given that morning, as if he had exclusive rights to them, we tend to forget all we have are gifts. The home in which we live, where some family may have lived before us and some may live after us; the food we eat, produced by someone with a greener thumb than ours; the talent behind our livelihood, given to us by a parent's genes and possibly passed along to our own children — all which is ours is not really ours. It's only on loan. And, considering who is the lender, is it any wonder we don't impress God as being able to have respect — respect-able?

If the odds of winning God's respect are stacked against us from birth, we don't help matters much. Not only do our obvious sins lose us our good name before God's judgment throne, but half the time we can't even remember of what we're being judged!

We've just passed through the time of year when we assess ourselves. Work evaluations, 1040 forms, the mimeoed Christmas letter telling what we've done the past twelve months — there's a kind of sameness to the statements we make on each. What promotion and/or raise in salary did we get; which great projects did we tackle; where did we vacation; any gain or loss in number of dependents; any major purchases? Such are the categories by which society rates success, but that's not how Christ rates us.

Last week I was filling out, in triplicate, a survey for the church — answering such questions as: have you recently started any new programs, gotten any more schooling, changed any basic theological positions? I had a great urge to send the questioner a "sensitivity survey" which Dr. Robert McCracken once composed! It asked — "Have you a quick eye, an outgoing nature, a heart tender and sympathetic? Do you care when others are hurt? Are you swift to sense their hurt and to do what you can to relieve it? Is anything human alien to you?" (McCraken, et. al. *The Riverside Preachers,* p. 71) Those were the traits of Jesus and the early Christians — quick eye, tender heart, eagerness to help, and be involved with all kinds of people. This is the core of the ministry of Christ—to visualize the deepest needs of people and, with them, be sensitive, supporting, and serving. As theologian, Jacques Maritian, has said, "The greatest truth of Christianity is that hearts are worth more than minds, muscles or money."

If God does not respect us, it may be because we have too few of his values to respect. Then again, it may just be God doesn't care what our successes are or what we like to brag about.

The phrase of Peter's we refer to as "no respecter of persons" literally means "does not take at face value." God isn't interested in the *face* we present to the world, as much as he's concerned with the *soul* we present to him. He doesn't dwell on what people think of us; he dwells on what he can do for us, and what he can do *with* us. What he promises to do is rearrange us, knock us down as the respectable people we like to think we are, and build us up as the servant-saints he needs us to be. Jeremiah called God the master potter and that's exactly how he works, taking the clay pots we once were content to be, breaking them up, and remodeling them in his fashion. Look at the heroes of the Bible — Moses, a prince of Egypt, whom God broke down into a stuttering shepherd on the run from the law, before he built him into his greatest prophet; Jacob, the conceited, rich patriarch whom an angel of God literally had to beat up before the Lord thought him ready to bear the title, Israel, prince of God; Paul, blessed with being both a Roman citizen and a Jewish Pharisee, whom God struck down, dumped in jail countless times, and then sent out simply as a Christian. Stand them up, these heroes of faith, and we'll honor them, but it surely will not be for the same things they were honored before God fashioned their lives.

So it goes even today. If God makes no distinction between Jews and Gentiles, man and woman, free man and slave, as St. Paul says, he'll certainly not go by society's standards in choosing people to bless, people to love, people to use in ministry. That was Peter's remarkable insight when he explained to Cornelius the significance of the resurrection: "Everyone who believes" — not just the Jews, not just the successful — but "everyone who believes in Christ receives forgiveness of sins through his name." For when God "does not take us at face value," it's because he's more concerned about us as unadorned father, neighbor, companion on the downtown bus, where career and titles are nameless. Such are the times, when our true natures come out, the only natures worth respecting. Those are the times when you make a meal for a friend who's sick, listen to the boring tale of a neighbor who needs an ear, help the kids with their homework, or say a prayer for the cousin who just married. Those are the times when you show your face beneath your face. Peter's description of God's people is just that stark in its simplicity — "any one who fears him and does what is right is acceptable to him."

When we allow ourselves to be such God-fearing, right-doing people in the daily affairs of life, we may be surprised, because we'll no longer be so eager to gain the world's respect. Our Bic pens can again be for writing, our Sears shirts can go unadorned, and we can walk in our boots without tripping. For the peace which comes from being valued by God and loved by God's people will be more priceless than all the worldly respect we can ever earn.

Preaching Your Life

Stories about preachers and preaching are endless. There's the famous preacher's lament: "I don't mind that people look at their watches while I preach; I just wish they wouldn't shake them to see if they're still running." Then, this sermon observation: "Sometimes a minister is asked to say something. Sometimes he has something to say. Occasionally the two coincide." And, of course, the preacher's prayer: "Lord, fill my sermon with good stuff, and stop me when I've said enough."

The implication in all of these stories is the same. Beneath the humor is the feeling that sermons are often windy with little content. And that's sometimes true! In an age when the average American is daily bombarded by scores of slick messages from full time, professional writers — T.V. shows, magazine articles, billboards — the words from the pulpit can seem pretty dull. The average preacher, after all, is a jack-of-all-trades who enters the pulpit with fear and trembling — or should.

Then, too, some sermons are moralistic and we turn them off because they sound like lectures from an angry schoolmarm. If someone talked to us that way outside of church, we'd even know the phrase with which to snap back: "Don't preach at me!" It's not easy being a preacher. It's not easy communicating God's Word by mouth.

I wonder if Peter knew what he was beginning when he preached the first sermon of the Christian church. Since that Pentecost morning, when he addressed the crowds in the street of Jerusalem, the twenty-minute pulpit ritual has become an institution in the church. However, it's an institution many people think has passed its prime. So how can we find God's Word alive and real in our lives? If sermons are so often disappointing, how can we find a vital faith?

I envy Thomas in today's Gospel. For a week he had been hearing from the other disciples how Jesus had risen from the grave. But hearing wasn't good enough. For Thomas, seeing was believing. And, in a miracle, Thomas did see. On this day, Christ appears to him, speaks to him, holds out his hands to him. Thus Thomas believes: "My Lord and my God!"

Does this mean we must have a vision of God to have genuine faith? If so, who could ever believe? Only a few mystics over the centuries have claimed such a visible encounter with God. Even Christ downplayed the idea when he said, "Blessed are those who have not seen and yet believe."

If we are to believe in Christ, we will have to be led by what we hear. And what we hear that moves us most and leads us farthest toward faith is the confession of faith by others, people who claim their lives have been shaped by Christ. Peter told the story of Jesus, in this Pentecost sermon, and could claim "of that we all are witnesses." Then he could give personal affirmation of belief as the clincher — "Let all the house of Israel therefore know assuredly that God has made him both Lord and Christ, this Jesus whom you crucified." The sermon is largely a confession of faith of the preacher — my faith — to which you can respond yea or nay. It's a self-disclosure in words and like other self-disclosures in words — "I love you," "I hurt," "I believe" — it begs a reply, begs you to take a stand, and, it is hoped, share that personal faith.

Faith begins in us when we hear others speak of their faith — the pastor, a Sunday school teacher, a parent, a college roommate. Their words may be awkward, their thoughts simplistic, but a message gets across. And more than a message — an enthusiasm, joy, or fire is conveyed. More than hearing simple statements of belief, you sense a spirit which can be shared. Our faith is more caught than taught.

And what's the content of that talking? A story. That's it — telling a tale, the *Greatest Story Ever Told* as the old movie title put it boldly. This is what gives faith substance and makes it intelligible from one person to the next. The Good News of Christ, whether preached from a pulpit or chatted across the back fence, is less a matter of teaching ideas than inviting to enter the story of Christ.

teaching ideas than inviting to enter the story of Christ.

Peter knew that. Notice the simplicity of Peter's sermon. Before his statement of faith, he simply tells the story of Christ — his ministry, death, and resurrection and his relation to David. There's no emotional harangue, no listing of do's and don't's, no anecdotes or jokes to maintain the hearers' interest. Only a narrative with which they can identify. If his confession of personal faith is the preacher's summons to faith, the story of Christ's life is the substance of that faith.

Larry Richards has said, "Christ never asks to share our lives. He invites us to share His." *(Is God Necessary?* p. 11) This is what all preaching, indeed all speaking of faith needs to be — not an argument to persuade you to believe, but an invitation to join the story of Christ. Our own stories are imperfect, laced as they are with fears, and defeats, and only those successes which leave us empty inside. Yet, each of us is only the sum of our experiences, our story — Mom and Dad's divorce when you were five taught you to be suspicious of love; making straight A's one High School semester gave you confidence and self-respect; losing a good job and how it triggered fear and tightened belts.

Our experiences shape us. We hope the good memories, the healing and building memories, outweigh the bitter, scarring ones. But there's no guarantee; the flaws are scratched into you forever.

Then comes Christ. His invitation is to expand our memories to include his experiences, to expand our life stories to include his life. "Christ never asks to share our lives. He invites us to share his." Christ is the archetype of our lives Paul promised the Corinthians when speaking of the resurrection (1 Corinthians 15:20 ff) The story of Christ becomes the heart of the story of each of his followers. Paul writes the Colossians: "As you received Christ Jesus the Lord, so live in him . . . In him you were also circumcised . . . and you were buried with him in baptism . . . also raised with him through faith . . . (and) made alive together with him." (Colossians 2:6-13)

You know what it means to "live in another." We do it when we watch a movie and identify with the hero. We do it when we go to a ball game and root for "our team" as if somehow we possessed them. We have a sense of vicarious experience — that these people on the screen or on the field are living on our behalf and their fate is ours. It's the same with adopting Christ's experiences as our story, except for this — Christ isn't pretending and neither are we. His agonies we've all shared to some degree; his triumph will be ours, too, and is already.

The atonement — the at-one-ment with God — means Christ lived, died, and rose again on our behalf, not simply as a substitute to spare us the ordeal, but as a representative to teach us what living, sacrificing, and triumphing really mean.

And this is why we share the Eucharist. In the bread and wine, Christ enters us. He gave himself for us not only on the cross; he gives himself to us each time we commune. In communion we are "in common" with him. Our identities blend.

Our lives are not destined for disappointment because of the frustrations, failures, and sins which haunt us daily. We are more than our personal histories. Christ's history is ours, too. His life teaches us how to live. His victory of Easter offers hope that we, too, will find eternal life beyond the grave. Your life is not the sum of your story — his story has to be added.

The purpose of preaching is to tell you that portion of your story lived by Christ. A dignified elderly lady first helped me see this. A few Sundays after I was installed in my first parish, I preached a sermon which I thought had all the marks of great oration — at times witty, at times forceful, with pacing and grammar impeccable. After the service this lady came to me and, with a single phrase, both deflated and inspired me. "Pastor," she said, "we would see Christ."

We would see Christ. Since Peter, on that Pentecost, first talked in the crowded street of Jerusalem, this has been why we preach and why we listen — to know Jesus better and to trust him more.

This morning I stand before you, not to entertain or impress but simply, like Peter, to share my faith and to repeat the story of Christ, "a man attested to you by God with mighty works and wonders and signs . . . killed by the hands of lawless men . . . this Jesus God raised up." I'm here to preach your life. For the heart of faith is for you to say yes to this as your story, too. In it you can find yourself. Its memories can shape your values; its triumphs can give hope to your future. Christ has lived this story in our place, so we need not live it but only learn it as our own.

58

Repent!

I didn't want to be in prison that day, even if I was only a visitor. Angry scowls or dull eyes followed my march down the hollow corridors and, at the end of each hall, I silently counted the number of locked doors behind me to the sunlight. Still, the phone call had said a friend of a friend was here and wanted to talk to a minister. And after all, visiting the prisoners was one of the commands St. Paul had given us. So, armed with caution, I had come.

The prisoner and I were left alone in a small room. After a few awkward moments of silence and some polite probing from each of us, his barrage of words began. Seated on cracked plastic chairs without even a table to separate us, he unloaded his thoughts — sorrow for his crime and for the embarrassment to his family, anger at the years taken from him, fear for the future, determination to go straight — words and feelings poured out of this usually quiet and dignified man. When they were through, he sat huddled, chin on chest, drained of words and emotions.

It's hard to face a broken man. It's embarrassing and somewhat unnerving because it reminds us we all are broken in some way. We all put on, for the world, a face we know is a little phony, a face that hides, with mascara or a smile, a lifetime of frustration and anger, worry and guilt. Showing the face beneath the public face is an act of courage or desperation or both. As I told this slouching man in the starched T-shirt of God's love and forgiveness, I found myself, also, speaking of my admiration for him. In looking deeply at himself and his failures, he had risked much. Maybe this admirable courage is why I was a little humbled when I walked out of that prison. Next time I thought of life behind wire cages and steel doors, I would not be so quick to condemn and fear.

Repentance is not a common word in our vocabulary. Confessing your sins and promising to go straight is a rare quality in prison. It's almost as rare in many churches. Today mainline Protestants treat the notion warily. Repentance is for Catholics with their sacrament of Confession and Absolution in those little booths where you recite your sins to an unseen priest and he tells you how many "Our Father's" to say to make things right with God. And repentance is for fundamentalists with their altar calls and fervent promises to start a new, *saved* life. But who speaks of repentance for congregations such as ours? Repentance was given a bad name by those cartoons of long-haired, wild-eyed old men carrying placards demanding *REPENT — THE END IS NEAR*. It's embarrassing, this repentance. It's foreign to us. That's why we feel out of our element before the Bible's repetition of the word.

Yet it's there in page after page of the New Testament. The one feature which haunts every sermon of Christ and his followers is the demand to confess your sins and promise to reform. Ragged John the Baptizer screamed it in the desert: "Repent, for the kingdom of heaven is at hand." Sophisticated Paul reasoned it on the steps of the Acropolis: "Repent, because (God) has fixed a day on which he will judge the world in righteousness." After his listeners had been "cut to the heart" by Peter recounting Christ's sacrifice, he made the demand as the exclamation point of his sermon: "Repent and be baptized every one of you in the name of Christ Jesus for the forgiveness of your sins."

In the language of the Bible, the Greek word for repentance means *turn around,* completely change your direction in life and, therefore, change your life itself. Repentance is not the same as regret. The Bible occasionally mentions people, such as Judas Iscariot, who regret their sins but it doesn't say they repented of them; usually their regret leads only to an early grave. People who repent seek new goals and new resolve to reach those goals. Perhaps we've kept the word foreign to us because it is so demanding, seeking to turn drunks into teetotalers, swindlers into Sunday school teachers. It was for good reason the convict I visited had cold sweats every moment he was spilling his guts. He had an entire life to remake. But you and I don't want that pain.

Also, repentance may be foreign to us because we're not sure we need it. We have made little mistakes, perhaps, but we've committed no murders, no embezzlements. We're not in the major league of sinners.

Wasn't that also true for those New Testament crowds to whom Jesus and his followers preached? The common feature to all of the congregations hearing those first sermons was they were average people. They were not labeled as culprits in any great crime, or members of any heinous society. Even when Peter said to his audience, "Jesus . . . you crucified," he pinpointed no one, but talked of people in general. These were upright Jews before Peter in Jerusalem, and noble Greeks before Paul in Athens, and pious Jews before John in the desert. Many had lives filled with no great sins, nothing major to apologize for. They had lives filled with nothing special. But then this was precisely *what* needed repentance — lives filled with nothing special.

A while ago I listened to an interview with Ann Longstreet on National Public Radio. Most of us have forgotten who Ann Longstreet is, but in the early 1960's she was a promising young writer — a female Hemingway, some said. Then Ann Longstreet stopped writing. The interviewer, that evening, kept pressing the question why no more stories from her pen? Each time he did came another excuse — marriage, the raising of children, the little things of keeping house, a simple urge to live life rather than reflect on it. Still the correspondent was unsatisfied and still he looked for a good reason. Then came a remarkable moment for nationwide radio — in mid-sentence Ann Longstreet fell silent. Like a culprit convicted of a crime, she could no longer make up excuses. From the radio came only faint sobs.

Our lives may not be ugly with sins that could make the newspaper, but we all have something to repent. For some, it's a talent wasted or a noble dream abandoned or a depression they can't shake. Some can no longer visualize themselves as the heroes in their own life stories. For most, there are moments of gnawing emptiness when they know something is wrong with life but can't identify it.

Here are the sins of the average person, the sins we need to repent. They are the sins of despair, doubt, prejudice, of facing life as a pointless routine. The fear-filled hesitancy of this jail chaplain needs God's forgiveness as much as the crime of the convict. The word repentance comes from the Latin word *paena* which means inner pain; therefore, all we do or don't do that troubles our souls and keeps us awake at night cries for our repentance. The life which drifts aimlessly needs to be turned around just as desperately as the life leading to jail.

The New Testament acknowledges the need to turn from this inner suffering when it speaks of hell. Most of the New Testament's references to hell are not to a fiery cosmic prison in the next life. They refer to a living hell, the turmoil within us now while we live. When St. Paul asserts, "the wages of sin *is* death," he is saying we are not so much punished *for* our sins later as we are punished *by* sin now.

How do we escape this inner punishment of guilt, loneliness, and worry? One way is by changing our lives. Part of repentance is changing; we can find inner health as we reform outer habits. Repentance involves developing new styles of living, acquiring new habits such as —

> using the living room as a place to talk with loved ones instead of a place to hibernate with the T.V.;
>
> deciding the purpose of your life, for the next ten minutes, is understanding and helping the man yelling at you;
>
> mowing the grass of the next-door neighbor you can't stand;
>
> giving some of the money you've banked to a charity so you both might be blessed;
>
> starting the day with devotions rather than a mental list-making of the drab chores facing you.

We measure our repentance by our reforms.

Yet beware of repentance as a quick fix. Changing actions without cleaning the heart does no more good than changing bandages without cleaning the wound. Before it is a changing, our repentance must be a confessing. Only when we painfully acknowledge our sins to God and to our loved ones will we take reforming seriously. More importantly, only as a broken, confessing people will we recognize the love of God we had blocked out before.

In Victor Hugo's classic *Les Miserables,* the escaped criminal, Jean Valjean, after living prosperously for many years under an assumed name, learns another man has been identified as him and charged with his crimes. After struggling with his conscience, the real criminal confesses his identity in court. Then, to his stunned friends, he explains: "You consider me worthy of pity . . . I consider that I am to be envied. What I do at this moment God beholds from on high and that is sufficient."

The purpose of repentance is this — God can again behold us from on high and we can realize we are known. By itself, confession cannot make us God's radiant, confident people. But it is the necessary prelude. It strips us of the false faces by which we've tried to hide from God and others and ourselves. Frederick Buechner said it well: "To confess your sins to God is not to tell him anything he doesn't already know. Until you confess them, however, they are the abyss between you. When you confess them, they become the bridge." *(Wishful Thinking,* p. 15)

In the end, repentance begins with nothing more and nothing less than being honest with God. He calls us to strip away the layers of pride and excuses and stand before him as emotionally naked as on the day he made us. That's both painful and frightening. But only when we do this, is there the possibility of finding the miracle of the cross — this God who could give his Son to die for us still loves us as much now, after a lifetime of failures and sins, as when he gave us birth as symbols of promise. Only as penitent people can God's understanding love be real to us. Long before we were ready to repent he was ready to forgive. And in the humility of our confession, we will find this is not so much the God of vengeance as the God of love, and, therefore, the source of peace and joy.

God's Passion

There is a short ditty,
> hardly good enough to be called a poem,
> but fun nevertheless.

> *Death reigns;*
> *With furrowed brows and sad eyes,*
> *All men live under darkened skies.*
> *Cold and lonely the days crawl by;*
> *In depression and doubt we all lie.*
> *Then the wind picks up, the sun breaks out;*
> *Come laughter and joy of which all men shout.*
> *In only days Winter dies,*
> *And in its wake Spring arrives.*

Such a flirtation with spring is upon us now. And with it comes an amazing transformation of spirits — spring fever. The effect of the malady varies — a longing for the golf course or, perhaps for a hammock; an urge to clean house or to pour through a seed catalogue, a revived love for the out-of-doors, a revived love for almost everything. In a few short weeks, the world is transformed.

That same spring fever was felt the year of the resurrection. Today's Scripture presents an eye-popping description of the transformation. First, John's Gospel describes the winter which lingered that first Easter night — disciples huddling together, living in fear, locking their doors; disciples, knowing deep down Christ's body was stolen and wondering whose boldness concocted the resurrection rumor.

Then, the transformation: Jesus appearing; Thomas confronted;

64

everyone believing. And the result of the Son/Sun's return? Good
times, which the church had never seen before or since. Listen to
Luke describe, in the book of Acts, Christianity's first spring:

> *They spent their time learning; sharing in fellowship meals*
> *and prayers. Many miracles were done . . . everyone filled*
> *with awe. All believers continued in close fellowship . . .*
> *shared their belongings . . . sold their property and posses-*
> *sions and distributed the money among all . . . Had their*
> *meals together . . . glad and humble hearts . . . praised God*
> *. . . enjoyed the good will of all the people. And everyday*
> *the Lord added to their group those who were being saved.*
> *(Acts 2:42-47)*

These are amazing words. The early church has long been the
example of what church life should be. Indeed these past 2000 years
we've judged our churches on how closely they resemble that gathering in Jerusalem, with all its simplicity, devotion, and warmth.

Much of our common history is a story of imitation of the early
church. We tithe in our offerings because they tithed. Many churches
have gone back to loaves of bread and jugs of wine for communion
rather than pasteurized grade drink and doughy "poker chips"
(wafers) because that's what Peter's people used. Our worship service comes directly from theirs; even our covered-dish dinners are
based upon their communal meals.

And such imitation is good and it's useful in describing the god-
ly life. But let's beware. There's something else which infested the
early church — something that gave the church its zing. It cannot
be imitated; indeed, it can hardly be described, though it shoulders
more descriptions than any other phenomenon of life. You see, the
early church was in love.

Let me explain. The language of the Bible has many words for
love. Three are most common: 1. *philos,* which means friendship
or brotherly love. From it we get Philadelphia, city of brotherly love,
and philosophy, love of wisdom. 2. *eros,* romantic love, alias puppy
love, "true love," and head-over-heels love. 3. *agape,* divine love,
the gentle love of a parent for a child.

In the Bible, divine love, agape love, holds center stage. Friendship love plays a strong supporting role. And romantic love? Well,
it's no more than a bit actor.

But this chapter of Acts is different. The contented joy of the church after Easter is the blissful self-surrender of new love. It was not spring fever the church felt; it was romance with God. For a change, God's love is not the quiet, respectful obedience of an Israelite nation to Yahweh after the Exodus. Nor is it the somber devotion of an Abraham toward a God for whom he's about to sacrifice a son. Rather, this love is the exuberance of a David, dancing as he brings God's altar into Jerusalem. This love is the joy of Jesus, laughing at the wedding in Cana. More than anything else, the warmth and happiness of the church after Easter is like the awe of a teen-ager awakening the day after his/her first serious date. For the first time in their life, they know they are loved.

Theologian Robert Capon explores this early church joy which we so readily envy. "God's approach to us," Capon writes, "becomes, not the orders of a superior directing what a subordinate must do, but the longing of a lover for what the beloved is. It is a desire, not for a performance, but for a person; a wish, not that the beloved will be obedient, but that she will be herself — the self that is already loved to the distraction." (Capon, *Hunting The Divine Fox,* p. 38) God responds to us, "not 'in order to' anything, but 'because of' someone."

It's not a new idea, this notion that God seeks us like a lover; it's as old as the biblical book, Song of Solomon. This writer says of God: "By night I sought him of whom my soul loveth . . . Tell me, O thou whom I love, where you journey . . . Why should I be as one who desires your friends? . . . Stay with me, comfort me, for I am sick in love."

It's not a new idea, but it is an insightful idea. Of course, we have usually looked on the love of God for us as the love of a parent for a small child. But this love has another side, too. How much truer, and more humbling, to recognize God seeks us because, in his own mysterious way, he sees us as lovable. And how much more exhilarating to return that love with the same rapture, rather than as a sense of duty.

Without understanding the early Christians were "in love," the details of early church life seem extravagant. However, their relations toward each other, and toward God, seem very familiar to anyone who's been "head over heels."

Lovers go to dinner and a show; Christians took communion whenever possible.

Lovers give expensive gifts; Christians sold all and gave it to the church.

Lovers are eager to know all about their beloved; Christians spent their time learning from the apostles.

Lovers whisper soft words to each other; Christians eagerly shared in prayers.

As for Acts' words, "They enjoyed the good will of all the people," well, "everybody loves a lover."

As Father Capon puts it: "The grandest — and the final — imagery the Bible uses for God's love is precisely that of lover and beloved, bridegroom and bride. It is the marriage of Christ and the church which is the last act of the long love affair between God and creation." (Capon, p. 39)

"A love affair between God and creation." This is what the early church knew, and what gave it such vitality. And if that seems distant and foreign, remember the marriage is 2000 years old now. Like all old romances, it may be hard to understand, a distant memory of freer times.

But it can be more than a memory. Through the years, God calls Christians to renew the passion for his presence which we once knew so clearly. He calls his people to renew it as a passion, and not a mere imitation of early church habits. It's the call he gave to Peter and Augustine and Luther; their faith was rooted deeply and attained great heights because they knew God offered and asked for a love that is passionate and not merely obedient.

And it's the call he gives us. Through the mystery of communion, through the exaltation of Easter hymns, through the excitement of spring, he invites us to open ourselves to the power of his presence.

He promised to overwhelm us with a love greater than any lovers.

For his love "is strong as death . . .

Its flashes are flashes of fire, a most vehement flame.

Many waters cannot quench his love, nor floods drown it."

(Solomon 8:6-7)

For those who dare fall in love with him, that power and passion is God's promise.

Practicing and Preaching

This morning's First Lesson from Acts is about a man who could have made the Bible's Guinness Book of Records twice. We remember St. Stephen as the first Christian to be martyred for his faith. He was an outgoing man whose eagerness to tell others of Christ got him in trouble with the Jewish authorities. They had him killed.

Just as importantly Stephen was the first Christian deacon. Actually Stephen wasn't expected to be preaching Christ at all. His job was as an administrator, not a pastor. Of more significance than how Stephen died was how he lived. For this man was a crucial member of the early church, although he had no credentials as disciple, apostle, or cleric. What was important about Stephen — and significant for us today — is told as a story earlier in the book of Acts. It's a watershed event in the life of the church.

Imagine the scene. So rapidly had the church in Jerusalem been growing the Christians had long since moved out of the small homes in which they had met each night for dinner. Now they meet in a social hall which strives to be a family-style restaurant, but is degenerating into a soup kitchen.

Scurrying about are the waiters — Philip and Matthew, Bartholomew and Nathan and most of the other disciples, juggling stacks of dishes in their fishermen's hands and undoubtedly dropping many of them. In the center stands maitre d' Peter, so busy telling stories about Jesus that he never sees the line of people standing at the door waiting to be seated. In the corner is James, shuffling from one foot to the other. Peter may be the center of attention, but James is the proprietor of the place. As Jesus' brother he's been appointed *Bishop* of Jerusalem. But he knows no more than the rest how to run a restaurant.

.

68

Finally comes the explosion. "My widowed mother didn't get dinner!" explains someone in Greek.

"We're not charging enough to make ends meet!" says another.

"The food's burnt," comes another Greek voice.

Leave it to the sophisticates who speak Greek to complain.

"Enough!" says Peter, throwing up his hands. "Find someone else to do the cooking and serving. That's not the job of disciples."

Then comes the watershed event. Stephen and six other level-headed laypeople are quickly elected to run the meals. They roll up their sleeves, grab some aprons, and jump in, never realizing they have become the world's first church council.

But St. Paul realized it. About twenty years later he writes of their work and says: "There are different kinds of service, but the same Lord . . . different kinds of working, but the same God who works in all . . . The Body is a unit, though it is made up of many parts . . . (and) you are the body of Christ and each one of you a part of it...apostles, teachers, healers, administrators, helpers . . . " (1 Corinthians 12:5-10)

Luther, too, realized the importance of this election of Stephen and the others. The slogan he gave their movement was "priesthood of all believers," which is another way of saying you don't have to be a pastor to minister.

What Peter has recognized and what Paul and Luther later restate is laypeople are as important to God's church as ministers. Paul says a body filled with eyes but with no ears, nose, or mouth would be as strange as it is useless.

There's only one problem with this emphasis on the importance of lay ministry. Most people don't believe it.

A while ago I attended a three-day seminar at a nearby seminary. While there I stayed with a friend of a friend, a young man my age named Bob. Bob is in his first year of preparing for ordination. For eight years he was a high school history teacher and had established a reputation for brilliance — he could motivate the most intransigent and expand the horizons of the slowest. Bob was also a dedicated Christian layman; he taught Sunday school, served on council, and was adored by all. Therein lay the problem. People could not resist the temptation of telling Bob, "Any young man, as dedicated to the church as you, should be a pastor." Finally he couldn't resist the pressure, and entered the seminary. He's not wildly enthused about his preparation for ordination, but he'll make a good pastor. The tragedy is, he was a *great* teacher.

Peter did not ask for the appointment of Stephen and the others to do things the disciples simply did not have time for — unimportant things not worthy of disciples. Peter wanted them to perform functions which the disciples could not do well. They had bungled the administration of the church's welfare system; they didn't know how to feed the hundreds of people who came for dinner each night. So they turned to a group of people who could offer a ministry better than the disciples — laypeople.

Things haven't changed greatly in 2000 years. There still are many ministries for laypeople to perform; many of them still can be done well only by laypeople. Consider some of the ministries laypeople can do better than pastors.

Evangelism, for one. Unchurched people usually are very respectful to ministers who tell them about God and invite them to church. But they seldom hang on every word because it's easy to write off the evangelizing minister with the thought, "Well, it's his job — it's what he's paid to do." But when a layperson speaks of his or her faith, people listen because they know it comes from the heart.

Surveys show the importance of your evangelism work. Every survey asking new church members why they first came to their new church show, generally, the same result. About one in ten say they just wandered in, or the church building looked inviting. One in ten say they wanted to be part of the church's program or Sunday school. One in ten say they come because the pastors attracted them. All the rest — about seventy percent — come because a friend or relative invited them or brought them.

The value of the laity's personal speaking of faith was recognized in the book *The Total Image: Selling Jesus In The Modern Age.* Author Virginia Owens writes, "It really is a very simple and obvious proposition I make: A person, whether human or divine, cannot be known — as a person rather than an image — except by immediate presence. If we want to project an image, either of Christians or the church, we can do that by means of television, magazines, books, billboards, movies, bumper stickers, buttons, records, and posters. If we want people to know Christ, we must be there face-to-face, bearing Christ within us."

Our lesson from Acts says Christians were multiplying daily. There were not enough disciples to lead many people to Christ so quickly. Only laypeople could have done it.

Stewardship is another ministry depending almost entirely on lay-people. A sanctuary for worship, books for Sunday school, professional musicians, newsetters — almost all of the programs of the church are possible only when funds are available. The more you give, the more programs of ministry we can offer.

Many people consider the giving of money an embarrassing subject which should not be mentioned from the pulpit. They're often the same tight-fisted people who should be embarrassed by such a discussion.

The Bible is very forth-right in its mention of money. It claims we own nothing and hold all we have as a trust from God. The instinct to acquire that makes America tick made the prophets furious. Jesus, whom the Bible records more often talking about money than about prayer, said wealth always is one of two things — dangerous or damnable. To soft-pedal stewardship is to concede the field to mammon.

There are no luggage racks on hearses, goes the old adage. You can't take it with you. And why should we want do? After all, we are never more like God than when we give.

Last year, in our church, the average family gave only two and one-half percent of its income to the church. Imagine what ministries we could offer if everyone gave a tithe; ten percent of one's income was routine in Christ's day. Imagine what we could do if the average, in this church, was as high as the average of most Protestant churches — four percent. Imagine.

Worship is another ministry only laypeople can do. At the heart of our worship is the liturgy, a word that literally means "work of the people." A worship service often is compared to a theatrical performance with actors, a director, and an audience. Most people assume the minister is the actor prompted by God, the director, for the sake of the congregation, the audience. But that's not right. Worship literally means "worth ship" — the transferring of praise and natural worth to God. In truth, the *audience* of our worship is God. The people in the pews are the actors, who give God the glory in song and study. The minister is merely the director, who guides the people in their praises.

Your eager participation is essential if God is to be glorified in worship. You've heard Jesus' words, "Where two or three are gathered in my name, there am I in the midst of them." Usually we quote this merely to console each other when only a handful have turned out for a service and we expect a meek, awkward worship. Actually, the two or three Jesus referred to were people gathered for a counseling session. In worship, our Lord expects an assembly, the body of Christ, making a joyful noise. Just as coals must come together to make a hot fire, so must people assemble for a dynamic worship; we cannot do it in isolation. Our Lord wants those Christians in worship to know an enthusiasm and an openness to his Spirit. As St. Paul said, worship involves a willingness to "let the word of Christ dwell in you richly, teach and admonish one another in all wisdom, and sing psalms and hymns and spiritual songs with thankfulness in your hearts to God." (Colossians 3:16)

Aiding society is another ministry best done by laypeople, today as in Stephen's day. In our community that is because, in your daily work, you see more of the needs of society than a pastor can. In the world, that is because only dedicated church people can make a big difference in alleviating world-wide poverty and sickness. The government won't do it — the current administration in Washington has cut foreign aid to less than ten percent of what it once was. Americans in general won't do it — among the twenty wealthiest nations of the western world America in the past quarter century, has gone from first, in our per capita giving to the poor, to dead last. Aiding the poor is another job only laypeople can do well.

Youth work is still another ministry best done by laypeople. It takes special gifts of talent, patience, and even charisma to lead youth into Christian living. The law of averages says those gifts will fall more upon some of the laypeople of the church than upon its pastors.

Evangelism, stewardship, worship and music, aiding society, youth work — these are your ministries, ministries which laypeople can do well. If you accept those ministries, then the same thing that happened to Stephen will likely happen to you. I don't mean you'll be stoned to death — few Christians make such a sacrifice today. I mean what happened to Stephen before his death. Remember? Acts says, "And Stephen (became) full of grace and power (and) did great wonders and signs among the people." So enthused did he become by practicing his faith, he couldn't resist gathering people to preach to them. In doing this he discovered the secret to a vital faith — acting in the name of Christ will lead to a fervent love of Christ.

My friends, I give you the same commission Peter gave Stephen. Accept the ministry God offers you. Accept it for the faith-lift it will give you. Accept it for what you can give him, his church, his world.

God in a Glimpse

Two nuns were returning to the hospital where they worked when they ran out of gas. They hailed a passing driver who said he would be happy to give them some — he could siphon it from his tank. The only problem was he had nothing to put the gas in. The nuns looked in their car but they found no container except a bedpan. This will have to do, they decided. So they filled it with gas from the man's car and waved goodbye as he drove away. As the nuns were emptying the bedpan into their gas tank, a trucker drove by. He slowed down, did a double take, and rolled down his window. As he passed he shouted, "Now that's faith."

Our Lord had a different idea of what faith is. We find him talking about it in the Gospel read several weeks ago when Thomas refused to believe in the resurrection unless he saw with his own eyes. "Have you believed because you have seen me?" asked Jesus, when he caught up with Thomas. "Blessed are those who have not seen and yet believe."

Believe without seeing — that is also Paul's message in our First Lesson this morning. Addressing the idol worshipers of Greece, Paul claims God is invisible. "The God who made the world and everything in it, being Lord of heaven and earth, does not live in shrines made by man, nor is he served by human hands, as though he needed anything, since he himself gives to all men life and breath and everything." Don't expect faith to come from a clear and simple hands-on experience with the Almighty, says Paul. God is much more elusive than that.

Faith is trusting in a God we cannot see or prove. It's a trust of his love and power. Faith is like the confidence of children in their father who carries them precariously on his shoulders. He never tells them he won't drop them — they simply trust. A placard in my office says it well — FAITH IS TO BELIEVE WHAT WE DO NOT SEE; AND THE REWARD OF FAITH IS TO SEE WHAT WE BELIEVE.

Believing without seeing is hard. Perhaps the most vexing problem of Christianity today is this one — how can we believe in a God who seems so invisible? In Jesus' day, at least, God seemed more evident. You could see Christ's miracles — the lame walking, the hungry fed, the dead sitting up. And one Jewish man out of ten had religion as a profession — teachers such as the Pharisees, ministers like the Levites and priests, monks like the Essenes. Everyone talked to and about God, so real was he to them. But God seems so quiet today. We pray for something, do not get it, and wonder if the Divine Giver is real. We watch science move steadily forward, conquering frontiers we thought belonged only to God, and we wonder just what is God's and where. We see world events lurch along chaotically, tragically, and we wonder if anyone up there is in control. Is there a Divine plan? Is there even a Divine Power?

Well, the Bible says there is. And Christ says there is. And the church throughout history says there is. Just because we can't see Jesus the way the disciples did, or hear a voice from God the Father as did Adam and Moses and the prophets, doesn't mean God isn't real. It simply means we haven't looked in the right places. Like Thomas, we were out the last time Christ passed by.

Let me suggest, this morning, that there are three ways we can glimpse this God who seems invisible. They are the three ways to faith.

The first way is by looking at his creation. We can't see God, but we can see the evidence of God. Look at his footprints passing through the universe. Look at nature, its intricate design and beauty of color and form — a flower, a snowflake, the atom, the Grand Canyon. How can one believe the universe was produced by a series of chance accidents rather than a master mind? When Paul said of God, "In him we live and move and have our being," he was claiming we are surrounded by the Almighty, if only we would recognize him, in the marvels of this world we take for granted. If we don't recognize him, it's because we can't see the forest for the trees.

Perhaps the most famous architect in English history was Christopher Wren. Wren died just before completing St. Paul's Cathedral, the second largest church in the world. St. Paul's was

Wren's masterpiece and represented his highest dream, so it was natural that he was buried in it. But he has no written memorial in the cathedral. Instead, a small plaque on his tomb says: "If you seek his monument, look around you." In St. Paul's, Sir Christopher Wren needs no monument. The cathedral is his monument because it bears more eloquent testimony to his greatness than any words of man. Isn't the same true for God, the architect of the world? As St. Paul said, "Ever since the creation of the world God's invisible nature, namely, his eternal power and deity, has been clearly perceived in the things that have been made."(Romans 1:20)

You can also see this evidence of God in the marvel of his highest creation, the soul and mind of man. Look at the conscience you find there, that inner urge telling us what we should do, and feeling gratified when we do it and guilty when we don't. In humankind's earliest novels, such as the *Iliad* and the *Odyssey* that inner voice we all have was unknown as a conscience — they called it the voice of the gods. They were not far wrong.

Think of the mind's awareness of an order to existence beyond our five senses, our ability to awe and wonder, our urge to worship so all civilization has some diety. How could this longing be just an unsatisfiable illusion? Hasn't God, instead, stamped his divine image on us? He made people, said Paul, "that they should seek God in the hope they might feel after him and find him." Our souls thirst because there is a God who can quench that thirst. We could only have longings because there is a God who can satisfy them.

If you struggle to believe in a God you cannot see, look at the evidence of him in his creation. It's as convincing as the scars in Christ's hands and side, and as tangible as idols made of gold.

You can't see God directly but, if you want to glimpse him, look at the transformed lives of some of his people. Saul of Tarsus was a mean-spirited bounty hunter of Christians, whom God knocked down and made over into his champion of love and faith, the Apostle Paul. Aurelius Augustine was a self-described liar, thief, and playboy, melted down and remolded by God as the brilliant theologian, St. Augustine. Giovanni Francesco Bernadone was a rich Italian soldier of fortune dubbed by his friends, "King of the Revellers," whom God transformed into the gentle and compassionate, St. Francis of Assisi.

If you want to see God you can glimpse him in his effect on people. And it's not only the *re*building of bad people into saints. Simple good people, like Martin Luther King, Jr. and Mother Teresa, he built into giants. And not only famous people evidence his touch. What about your neighbor who endures long hours and low pay as a social worker because he or she feels called by God to help others? What about the choir member with a new gleam in her eye and encouraging words to all since God cured her cancer? If you want to glimpse God, look at the enthusiasm of his people; enthusiasm literally means *"en theos"* — *God in them.*

I can recognize God's reality in his effect on my own life. During those stretches of days or weeks when my thoughts are taken over by work, family, and routines, but when God is ignored — stilted prayers, no study, no wondering what Jesus would be doing in my shoes — during those God-less periods I unconsciously become depressed, tired, living in a haze. But the more I devote myself to being with Christ in my mind, the more confidence, joy, sensitivity, and power I find. Isn't that what Paul meant when he said "It's not I who do these things, but Christ within me"? There's a well-known prayer that expresses well the power that God can exercise in our lives: "Help me to remember, Lord, that nothing's gonna happen today that you and I can't handle together."

This recognized presence of God even determines what we call our places of worship. Early Christians could so sense God's presence and might they called their gathering places "houses of power." The Greek word for that, *kuriakon,* has come down to us as "church."

With a faith longing for certainty, we look for God and do not see him. But we do see evidence of him in nature and we do spot his transforming power in his people. More than that, in the Gospels we meet him incarnate as Christ. The whole point of Jesus' ministry prior to his death was that we might know what God is like — what he thinks, how he acts, what he wants. When the disciples asked Jesus to show them God, he replied, "He who has seen me has seen the Father." (John 14:9) Here is the *sine qua non* of our search for God. To have faith in God means first to read the story of Jesus in the four Gospels, to read them as humble and honest seekers so Christ might reveal himself to us and make the Creator God real to us. As Jesus said, "No one knows the Father except the Son and anyone to whom the Son chooses to reveal him." (Matthew 11:27)

Therefore, in our search for God we can glimpse his evidence in his people and in nature and in Christ. And does that mean we can then believe in him? The irony is most of us can't then believe. At least, we can't believe based solely on the evidence. God doesn't work this way. He'll never be so evident that belief is inevitable. It's always up to us to accept him or not. It's the leap of faith. Faithfulness is not assenting to beliefs, but surrendering to a person we call Lord and Savior. And the result of faith is commitment, not credence.

Theologian Brooke Westcott wrote 100 years ago: "A Christian is essentially one who throws himself with absolute trust upon a living Lord, and not simply one who endeavors to obey the commands and follow the example of a dead teacher."

The good news is such a throwing of yourself on the Lord is not as difficult as you might fear. It's a leap of faith, true, but it's not across an impossibly wide chasm. For Christ promises *"Blessed* are those who have not seen and yet believe." And the heart of this blessing is that God himself will advance the faith-building if we can only say the initial, "My Lord and my God." As St. Mark puts it: "O God, I believe; help thou my unbelief."

Part of the responsibility for faith lies with you. We are like those Greeks to whom Paul preached — we haven't seen God so clearly that believing in him is easy and automatic. But we do see enough evidence of him and we have heard enough people who do believe that we, too, can say: "Lord, I believe. Help me to throw my whole weight on you."

A final story. When Holman Hunt painted his famous picture of Christ outside a door knocking, he showed his picture to a friend before it was publicly exhibited. The friend looked at the kingly Christ seeking entrance to the believers' home through the thick wooden door. Suddenly he said, "Hunt, you've made a terrible mistake here." "What mistake?" the artist asked. "Why, you've painted a door without a handle." "That's not a mistake," Hunt replied. "The door has the handle on the inside."

Acts 1:1-11
Ascension Sunday

Easter 7
Acts 1:6-14

Why Look To Heaven?

"A touch of Paradise" was her favorite expression and, in many ways, that romance with her was. It was a classic case of first love — for me, at least. She was an older woman — eighteen, I think, to my seventeen — and her emotions were sturdier since she had endured several romances before me. Maybe my rookie heart was why the touch of heaven I felt with her, so often felt like a strangle hold. She was outgoing and popular; I was insecure and shy. She coyly commanded; I awkwardly obeyed. My worth was as a reflection of her. That's the way it is with first love I've since learned. She became manipulative; I became passive. It's hard to understand why they call it love.

Two memories stay with me from that first big romance. One is my great relief that we never made it to the altar as we had dreamed back then. Those two confused teen-agers would have made a terrible marriage.

The other memory was of her *Dear John letter.* I kept it for years. With insight unusual for her, she wrote: "You cling too tight. You try so hard to live your life through me that you stifle us both."

That piece of wisdom almost makes my first love worth the pain. A person can cling too tightly to another. He can try to live his life through her, stifling her life and stunting his own.

I wonder if the same thing could ever be said of our love for God. Do we ever try to cling so tightly to God, living in Jesus' shadow, that we stifle our growth as God's children? Do we too often use our quiet walk with God to slip away from the world's problems and challenges?

There's no doubt the perennial problem of Christianity is our lack of intimacy with God. Too many people blithely sail through life ignoring God, except when they're ship-wrecked by some crisis and frantically send him an S.O.S. But today there is a growing resurgence of religion in America, a *revival*, with some people claiming born-again experiences and many people claiming increased devotion to their Lord. This is creating a new problem: Christianity as escapism.

I see it with the slide shows I offer on Israel and the life of Christ. Participants ask for more and more scenes of quaint fishermen sailing on peaceful lakes, quiet sheep grazing on green hills, and temple models gleaming white in the sun. Few are interested in descriptions of the sufferings of Christ or of the modern church's ministry in the Holy Land.

I hear the same echoes of escapism on the T.V. and radio. Religious disc jockeys love to tell stories about people who gave up their bad habits and struggles and accepted Christ. They play pop religious records wailing the word *Jesus* until the listeners almost enter a trance. Through it all, the message seems to be: you can leave the world behind when you enter the presence of Christ.

And that's disturbing. Are we to bury ourselves in the mystical presence of Christ?

Certainly that was not the message of the Ascension.

Luke paints a haunting picture of Jesus' last hours on earth. As the disciples journeyed with Jesus to the mountain, they asked if he was about to restore the Kingdom of Israel. The disciples wanted this dreamed-of land where Christ so obviously reigned, where there were no problems, everyone lived in comfort, and God protected the righteous. But Christ said, *No, they have to remain in the world.* Then, as they stood huddled together, came the great shock. Christ disappeared into a cloud. As the disciples, like lost children, stood gawking into the air, an angel appeared and said: "Why look to heaven?"

At the Ascension, the disciples sought to continue their lives in Christ's presence. And why not? They had known a good life — Christ had done the healing, the teaching, the confronting of enemies. The disciples had only to live meekly in a corner of that dynamic man's life. But no longer. Now God was telling them to go out into the world, go out to be the new healers and preachers and confronters. Like that awkward boy that I was, the disciples wanted to escape the world and live in the one they admired and loved. But they were turned away so they could mature as individuals.

Our faith speaks often of Christ as our comforter and shield. That image is good and it's true. But as any parent of a small child knows, solace and protection sometimes are not the healthiest things for a person. Sometimes giving freedom, giving the encouragement to experiment and grow on your own is the loving act.

This is what Christ offered at the Ascension. In a departure scene that was unnerving at the time, Christ offered the disciples — and us — the freedom and the opportunity to grow, to go from student to teacher, from follower to leader, from observer to healer. The key to the meaning of the Ascension is this switch in our roles. No longer are we to leave the world to be in Christ's presence; now we are to enter the world knowing Christ is present in us. "Lo, I am with you always, even to the end of the world."

The Ascension marks a dramatic shift in our relationship with God. Before the Ascension, as the Bible traces, the most dramatic acts of faith were the *entering into* God's presence: Abraham standing on the altar of sacrifice with Isaac; Moses nearing the burning bush and later receiving the Ten Commandments; Ezekiel falling on his face before God's awful majesty; David humbly entering the Holy of Holies in the Temple. After the Ascension, the dramatic acts of faith were the excursions into the world *on behalf of God,* the venturing forth confident God would be in us: Peter defying the authorities by preaching in the marketplace; Stephen performing miracles in Christ's name even though it meant his own death; Paul sailing to parts unknown to speak of God's Word. We see the change, too, in the images of faith which the Bible presents. While the Old Testament often pictures our faith as a walled city, a fortress in which we gain protection, the church after the Ascension frequently describes our faith as a ship in which we boldly venture into the world.

The new relationship with God that came with the Ascension is the difference between being a disciple and being an apostle. Certainly we are called to discipleship — to be students and followers of the master. But we're also called to apostleship. We're called to take the Good News we've learned from Christ and share it. And that's not just a selfless act. The shift in roles often prompts personal growth in us. When we seek to live "in Christ" we may be seeking to hide in Christ. Real growth comes when we allow Christ to live in us. Real growth comes when we as Christians venture forth into the world, when we attempt to change the world rather than escape from it, when we let Christ be our guide and healer rather than our protector. Look at the disciples. When they lived in the presence of Christ they were cantankerous, doubting, often shallow. After the Ascension, when they knew Christ was present in them through the Holy Spirit, they became giants. Peter changed from a stubborn, impetuous coward into a courageous leader; Thomas, the doubter, became the staunchest of believers; John, known before only for his gentle love, turned into the wisest of them all.

The key to this metamorphosis was the new purpose for living which Jesus gave his followers that day. "You will be my witnesses . . . to the ends of the earth." These students-turned-teachers had been given history's greatest gift — a personal knowledge and relationship with Christ. Their task now was to spread that gift. "Why look to heaven?" asked the angels. Start looking at people. Why stay on this mountain of ascension? Go now "to the ends of the earth." So the early apostles fanned out from Jerusalem to preach in the streets and homes of distant cities. Christianity grew because it was an outgoing *witness in* the world rather than a safe *retreat from* the world. And that's still the key to its success. Survey after survey shows of the new members of the average church, fewer than ten percent came initially because of some inanimate allure, a newspaper ad, perhaps, or the attractiveness of the church building. Over seventy percent came because some concerned Christian, some modern apostle, went out of their way to personally invite them. Christ called us to plant the seed of his Word. He said nothing about decorating and guarding the barn filled with the harvest of the faithful.

The key to this metamorphosis of the disciples was something else, too. God gave them his Holy Spirit. "You will receive power when the Holy Spirit has come upon you," Christ promised. The name he gave the Spirit literally meant the Encourager, the Prompter. He is a dynamic force which Christ promised would bring fulfillment to the lives of these disciples and empower their witness. He will give them a measure of the same divine force that animated Christ. But he is a Spirit they will know only when Christ has gone to Heaven.

The good news of this day is God did not leave us behind on that hill of ascension. As the Spirit, he goes with us to the ends of the earth, to help us more than hide us. He goes with us to help our adolescent faith mature in wisdom, courage, and love. For we are no longer to live in the shadow of Christ. Now we are to be the world's Christians, which literally means the world's "little Christs."

We are filled with the greatest power in the world and commissioned with the greatest task in the world. Is it any wonder angels still puzzle at our hesitation, and ask, "Why look to heaven?"